Published by **Becon**
an imprint
Enete Enterprises, LLC

6504 N Omaha Ave
Oklahoma City, OK 73116 (USA)

1st publication of
Becoming an Expat: Ecuador

Becoming an Expat *has filed for* Trademark™

Enete, Shannon 2014

Becoming an Expat Ecuador 2014 / Shannon Enete

ISBN-13: 978-1-938216-07-7
ISBN-10: 1938216075

Printed in the United States of America
www.EneteEnterprises.com

Becoming an EXPAT

ECUADOR

Shannon Enete

ECUADOR
2014

Becoming an EXPAT

ECUADOR 2014

Shannon Enete

OTHER BOOKS IN THE SERIES

 Becoming an Expat: **Costa Rica**

UPCOMING EDITIONS

Fall 2014: Thailand edition
Winter 2014: Brazil and Mexico Editions
2015: Panama, Belize

visit: www.Becominganexpat.com

- to see updates in-between editions
- for additional resources
- to discover what we come up with next!

To my wife, my adventure, hiking, and life partner, whose heart is where my home will always be.

DEDICATION

To all of my expat friends who have shared their experiences, helped to answer questions, and shaped this book with real life accuracy and a comprehensive experience. I'd like to give a special thanks to: Amy Prisco, Dr. Marcos Chiluisa, Ashley & Michel, Joel & Joanne, Connie & late *'Old Man'* Wilson, Bev & James Petersen, Carlene & Bill Chapman, Diane & Mark Bublack, and Stephen Aron.

TABLE OF CONTENTS

Set up Your Communication

After You Arrive

PART IV - Family & Education.......... 168

Moving with a Family

INTRODUCTION

I am not here to persuade you to move to Ecuador. No one country fits all, it's either right or wrong for you. My goal is to help you answer that question, and equip you if Ecuador is your sweet spot.

This book is comprised of my experiences, research, and a plethora of years of experience from numerous expats living across the country. The following words are not sugar-coated like other international lifestyle resources that attempt to sell you a dream. True to the *Becoming an Expat* series, you will read about the good, the bad, the stuff in-between, and the stuff you would never have thought of in a no-nonsense playful tone.

Ecuador (EC) is extremely affordable, full of freedoms and natural attractions. On the flip side of those liberties exist disorganization, latency, crime, and inefficiency. The side that you choose to focus on will directly relate to your happiness and overall experience living in the middle of the world. At least twenty-five percent of expats who make the move to Ecuador, return home within 3 years.

You'll notice that I have include a lot of additional resources via links or other books to read. The links are often "bitly" links for two reasons. One, they shorten the links, making them easier to input (sometimes the links are three lines long). Two, I can see what links you are most interested in, thereby learning how to serve you better in upcoming editions.

Keep an eye out for updates on www.BecominganExpat.com in-between editions since the ever-changing immigration laws, cost of living, and international experience is in constant flux. Also, look for videos, articles, and helpful resources on our website and Facebook Page: *Becoming an Expat*.

If Ecuador is one of many countries that you are weighing as your new home, look for our other editions "Costa Rica, Panama,

Thailand, Mexico, Belize, and Brazil." (Many of these editions are currently being constructed.) Also keep your eye out for supplemental *Becoming an Expat cookbooks, workbooks,* and video tutorials.

THE BASICS

All of the essential information needed to get you up and running towards or away from Ecuador

THE BASICS

THE A-Z TO A NEW COUNTRY AND CULTURE

In English, Ecuador (EC) translates to "equator" which slices the world in half separating the north from the south. Cultures have collided and intermingled for thousands of years here, creating an indigenous melting pot second to none.

The country is comprised of four regions: the Coast, the Galápagos Islands, the Sierra, and the Amazonia (which is also called the Oriente or east). Across these four regions, there are more indigenous communities and cultures represented than any other country in South America.

Commonly known as the *land of fire and ice (to be said in a deep radio announcer voice)*, Ecuador is home to a variety of climates with a financial climate of half that of the United States. Theoretically, you could live in your ideal climate year-round for half of the cost. You wouldn't be living the same life, however. *Becoming an expat* isn't shopping at outlet malls. You don't head home with the same product for less. Ecuador is a foreign country, so everyday tasks will be foreign until you learn to adapt to them.

Known for its safety and lifestyle, Ecuador is often described as what the US was like 30-50 years ago when one income could still sustain a family.

It is located in the northwest region of South America with Colombia to the north and Peru to the south.

HISTORY

Ecuador has worn many faces over the last 8,000 years. Seemingly similar to a bloody game of twister. The land and its people endured the following empires: pre-Incan, Incan, Spanish Conquest, Spanish Colonial, Colonial era, and Gran Columbia before it arrived to common-day Ecuador and its independence. Thousands of years and lives were spent over colonizations, clads, cultures, languages, religious, and lifestyle shifts to gain today's structure and self reliance.

The Manteños were the last pre-Columbian indigenous group that existed along the coast. Living from 600-1534, they were the first to witness the end. The end of an Incan era by the sight of the Spaniards' sails gliding their ships ashore with the intent to conquer.

The Manteños were excellent craft and seamen. They produced weaved goods, textiles, pearls, and articles of gold for trade. Common-day Manta was named after the group.

When Gran Colombia fell in 1830, Venezuela, Ecuador, and the common-day Colombia were formed.

After more than 70 years of independence, the Republic of Ecuador has lost territories from both its north and south. There is still pain hovering in the air over the loss of much of their Amazonian territories to Peru, which is evident from the recent border-war stemming from 1995-1999.

STABILITY

Compared to what? Stability can vary greatly depending on your definition.

Would five years of a peaceful regime be considered stable?

Ecuador has enjoyed over a decade of fairly stable democratic rule with three peaceful transitions of government. This is a big deal for a young country which has endured 100 governments and 20 constitutions. The current constitution was drafted in 2008. The branches of government have proven to lack an effective checks and balance system to avoid abuses of presidential power. Constant squabbles persist from coastal left-winged Guayaquil constituents to the conservative and rigid Andean highlands / Quito people.

MILITARY

The military in Ecuador has won a right to power in the government by the allocation of a number of seats in the Senate to military officers. This was accomplished in the constitution that was created after the military successfully ousted President Carlos Julio Arosemana Monroy in 1963. Over twenty years later the military warned the president of Congress, if the impeachment hearings against Febres Cordero were not halted, the military would shut down the legislature.

Expat, Connie Wilson with Salinas Officers

CRIME

Just like any country, crime is dependent on the region. Guayaquil has earned the reputation of the most dangerous city in Ecuador. Mind your belongings while in large cities. According to the OSAC (a United States Department of State Bureau of Diplomatic Security), pick-pocketing, purse-snatching, robbery, and hotel-room theft are the most common crimes committed against U.S. citizens. So don't leave your DSLR camera or bag in the back seat of your rental car!

Many towns in Ecuador are very safe, but you must be aware of the social economic differences that exist from North America. If you accessorize with jewelry and goods that could feed an Ecuadorian for over a year, you are dangling one hell of a carrot on your person. Be extra mindful of your belongings and leave flashy jewelry at home when traveling through bus terminals, big cities, and especially when hailing cabs in Guayaquil and Manta. Robberies by taxi, locally known as *"secuestro express"* are a growing problem. Hire a driver that you know, have a hotel call a cab for you, or rent a car to avoid this not-so-pleasant donation to the black market.

Also, credit card fraud is on the rise. If you wish to use a credit card, like I do to accumulate airline miles, accompany your card to the register. Never let it leave your sight. It's much harder to copy or make a slim (fake plastic replica of your card) with you supervising them.

If you're from the US, you might find this article[1] that compares reported crime between Ecuador and the US. It might provide some prospective. This document, of course, only represents documented crimes.

According to the mentioned OSAC, you don't have to worry about rambo-styled guerrilla activity or substantial political instability for that matter, which is more than their neighbors in Colombia can say. Colombia's mess spills over into northern Ecuador in the form of kidnappings, robbery, violent crime, and drug trade activities. So steer clear, or be extra wary of northern border towns.

If you are a victim of a crime, the OSAC says to:

"Immediately file a police report with the local authorities and to inform the American Citizens Services Unit at the U.S. Embassy in Quito or the U.S. Consulate General in Guayaquil. You may call the US Embassy Quito and ask for American Citizen Services: (02) 398-5000. If you are a victim of

---

[1] http://bit.ly/ecuscrime

crime, the U.S. Embassy or Consulate General can: help you find appropriate medical care for violent crimes such as assault or rape; put you in contact with the appropriate police authorities and contact family members or friends on your behalf; replace your stolen passport; and help you understand the local criminal justice process and direct you to Ecuadorian attorneys or law enforcement officials."

In case of an emergency, dial 911 in Quito and Ibarra, dial 112 in Guayaquil, Cuenca, and Loja, dial 101 everywhere else for police or 102 for ambulance and fire personnel. The Red Cross can be reached by dialing 131. Keep in mind these operators only speak Spanish.

For the latest security and threat information, see the Department of State's travel website (http:// travel.state.gov) and U.S. Embassy Quito's website (http:// ecuador.usembassy.gov).

Contact Numbers

US Embassy Quito
Switchboard:
+593-2-398-5000
Marine Security Guard Post One: +593-2-398-5200
Regional Security Officer:
+593-2-398-5475
Consular Affairs and American Citizen Services:
+593-2-398-5399
Embassy Duty Officer:
+593-997-883-222

Consulate General Guayaquil
Switchboard:
+593-4-232-3570
After-Hours: +593-4-232-1152
Regional Security Officer:
+593-4-232-8207
Consular Affairs and American Citizens Services:
+593-4-232-2758

SEX

The age of consent in Ecuador is 14 regardless of sex or orientation. Sexual crimes and assaults do exist. To avoid being a victim, never accept a drink or food from a stranger.

Also, never leave your drink or food unattended.

HIV is not a prevalent problem in Ecuador with only 0.3% of the population afflicted.[2]

ECONOMY

Ecuador exported more bananas than any other country in the world until they struck oil in 1967 in the Oriente. By 1973, oil had replaced bananas as the primary export of the country. They "drill baby drilled" their way into an unknown fluctuating market.

Ecuador's government borrowed heavily, believing the proceeds from the oil would repay their debts. Those same proceeds did not make it into many hands. Only a few pockets were able to capitalize on the funds, leaving Ecuador more broke and in debt than ever.

While they still export bananas, oil remains Ecuador's economic bread and butter. Because of this fact, each time the world price of oil drops as

it did in 2008, it wreaks havoc on their economy.

EXPAT QUOTE

Where do you see Ecuador in 5-10 years from today?
"I see an influx of foreign investments, more than North America (China and Russia). More Canadian and US expats retirees will make the move as the US and other expat spots become less affordable.

I also see the regulation here tightening up. The country is progressing but under the control of the government. If people move here because they don't like big brother, the same thing is going to happen here. Ecuador is moving from 3rd world to 1st world quickly. I hope they manage the growth well."
~ Amy Prisco
alprisco@gmail.com

The pursuit for oil has lead them to drastically disrupt the Amazon Basin. Indigenous tribes and rain forests that were previously sheltered are

---

[2] CIA World Factbook demographics statistics as of 2007

being disrupted with equipment that has no sensitivity to ecosystems.

Dollarization

A series of unfortunate events lead to the demise of Ecuador's currency, the Sucre. After seventeen years of political stability, El Niño destroyed much of Ecuador's infrastructure and export agriculture.

Rumichaca Bridge

This lead to a default on foreign debt, hyperinflation, and the eventual demise of the Sucre. The Dollarization wasn't a popular move. After President Mahuad turned to the Dollar to stabilize the economy, the indigenous and labor leaders protested and demanded Mahuad's resignation. They succeeded in forcing Mahuad to flee, but his successor was also a supporter of the Dollar, so I wouldn't go so far to say they won out.

With the addition of the Dollar to their economy, the rampant inflation was nipped in the bud, foreign investors interests were peaked, and long-term plans for economic growth were initiated.

The other side of the coin is not as shiny. Ecuador no longer has control of its money. All decisions about the currency are made thousands of miles away by another country. Plus, the problems that caused the Sucre to die a slow death are still alive and well. The government hasn't slowed it's spending or corruption.

The 2013-14 Global Competitiveness Report ranks Ecuador 71st out of 133 countries! That is 128 slots lower than the US rank. On the other side, they are up 15 slots from last year!

TIP

Large bills are impossible to use in Ecuador. $50 or $100 bills can only be changed out at the largest banks or the largest supers. Ecuador has seen more than its share of fraudulent $100s and because of this most establishments will not accept them even if they have ample change. Even $20 bills can be difficult to use around town.

CULTURE

Ecuadorians are open and friendly people. They enjoy their expat friends. The depth of friendship can vary depending on their abilities to communicate with one another. Their culture has deep roots in Catholic and indigenous traditions. They are conservative, but do not hold foreigners to their same beliefs.

The culture varies in each region of Ecuador. The coast is home to a relaxed, tranquil people. Guayaquil is filled with businessmen and women who are success driven and could be described as the New York of Ecuador. The Sierra and Amazonia regions are home to the most gentle people that Ecuador knows.

Ecuador's indigenous[3] population is arguably the most politically organized in the world! Two major confederations, Fonakin (Federación de Organizaciones de la Nacionalidad Kichwa de

EXPAT QUOTE

What are the best and worst parts about living in Ecuador?
"I think the best part is it's a lot more laid back, and there are less expectations. Now, expectation is a double edge sword. We come down with a North American mentality, when people show up for meetings a day late without apology, it gets frustrating."
~ Amy Prisco, expat since 2006 from New York City
alprisco@gmail.com

Napo) and Ashin (Asociación de Shamanes Indígenas de Napo) are located along the Amazon basin in Tena.

---

[3] A list of indigenous organization can be found here: http://bit.ly/ECindigenousgroups

HOLIDAYS

HOLIDAY	DATE
New Years	1 Jan
Carnival	early Mar
Maundy Thursday	Mar/Apr
Good Friday	Mar/Apr
International Workers' Day	1 May
Battle of Pichincha	24 May
Simón Bolivar's Birthday	24 July
Independence of Quito	10 Aug
Independence of Guayaquil	9 Oct
Dia de la Bandera	31 Oct
All Soul's Day	2 Nov
Independence of Cuenca	3 Nov
Quito was Founded	6 Dec
Christmas	25 Dec
New Year's Eve	31 Dec

GAY / LESBIAN

Welcome to a 95% Catholic nation. Well, that is, if you are straight, you are more than welcome. Homosexuals and transgendered persons are not offered the same legal protections as heterosexuals. This is not a new situation for LGBT folks from the United States. However, Ecuador is a bit behind the States regarding progress. Same-sex activity was illegal as recent as 1997!

My personal experiences in Ecuador as a married lesbian were not terrible but not ideal either. Most people I spoke with at length asked if my wife was my sister. They were confused when I explained that she was, indeed, my wife. It was as if their brain had already decided they liked us, but it didn't jive with this new information. After some contemplation, they usually came to the conclusion it was ok because we were from the States, but *that sort of thing doesn't happen in Ecuador"* or so we were told.

On a very positive note, in 1998 Ecuador became the first country in the Americas and the third country world-wide to include protection for sexual orientation in it's constitution.[4]

Quito and Guayaquil, the two largest cities in Ecuador, are the first two cities to have gay nightlife.

WATER

Take care to drink bottled water while in Ecuador. I would go so far as to say brush your teeth with bottled water as well until your body adjusts to some of the new bacterias. For the first month or two, I would also make sure and avoid fruits and vegetables high in water content such as: lettuce, watermelon, oranges, etc. Luckily, bottled water is cheap and readily available at your local super or pulpería (corner store). Many stores can arrange to deliver a large multiple-gallon jug to your home.

Water service is far from perfect. Fifty-percent of the urban areas experience water interruption, and water pressure is substandard. As far as waste

goes, a staggering 92% of wastewater is discharged into rivers and creeks without any kind of treatment!

FOOD

When I asked an Ecuadorian woman who served lunch about the soups I saw served everywhere, she explained, *"A lunch without soup is not a lunch at all."* You might think this strange for the coastal regions that boast 85-95 degrees F (29 - 35 C) with a tropical sun. Hot soup is an essential first course of lunch across the country. To counter balance the warm soup, a cool handmade

---

[4] Article 11(2)

fruit juice is served to accompany each *typical* meal. The main dish includes a plate of menestra (their typical red bean or lentil), rice, and a meat.

Like many countries in Latin America, Ecuador utilizes rice and beans as a staple. I did notice that while they have easy and dirt cheap access to veggies, they don't play a main role in Ecuadorian cuisine.

Other common foods include:
Churrasco: rice, french fries, slices of avocado, stir fried peppers with beef, finished off with a fried egg on top.
Ceviche: fish or seafood ceviche made in lime juice, red onion, and cilantro
Patacones: mashed green plantains that are deep fried and served with fry sauce or guacamole.
Guatita: cow innards (I was too chicken to try this one).

ALCOHOL

Aguardiente, translated *"fire water"*, is a sugar cane-based spirit rated at 60 - 100 proof or more if it's homemade!

It's often considered Ecuador's unofficial national drink. Canelazo is a drink often consumed in the Andes and is neighboring Colombia's national drink. It's a warm sweet and spicy drink created with boiling water, cinnamon sticks, aguardiente, lemon, and sugar. You may also run into *chicha*, made from fermented maize or cassava. This drink requires an adventurous soul because in order for the ingredients to ferment, they must first be chewed then spit back out!

LANGUAGE

If your native tongue is anything other than Spanish, the above mentioned alcohol might be needed to help loosen your tongue to converse with the locals. It is true, Ecuadorians do indeed speak Spanish. In addition to Spanish, Quechua, an indigenous Amerindian language is often spoken. In fact, there are nine separate Quechua dialects spoken by 1,460,000 people across the country.

While there is some English spoken in touristy areas such as: Quito, Cuenca, and Baños, your stay will be infinitely more enjoyable, and every day tasks more doable, if you learn Spanish.

CLIMATE

Ecuador has a variety of climates that vary depending on how close you are to the beach, equator, or how high you are in the mountains. The coast is hot and wet, particularly between January and April, average day highs in the 80s F (26 C).

The mountains range from perfect and 70 F (21 C) all day to *chilly*! Keep in mind that heaters are not the norm here. Quito averages 66 F (19 C) during the day and 50 F (10 C) at night. Wet season visits from October through May. See more about regional climates in the **Where is Your Haven** section.

NATURE

Ecuador is merely the size of Nevada and yet is home to an impressive range of landscapes: the Andes, Amazon, Galapagos Islands, and twice as many birds as the continental United States! Ecuador also wins the battle for most plant species when compared to the much larger US.

Conservation is not among the forefront of thinking, however, it's there somewhere lurking. The country has protected 18% of its land, but at the same time lives by the slogan "Drill baby drill." Deforestation and oil exploitation are real problems.

Cuicochi Lake, near Cotacachi

TRANSPORTATION

BUS EXPERIENCE

The buses are designed for a person statured 5'6" or less, US children sized individuals, or adults that are about 5'4" (*most Ecuadorians I observe are between 4'10"-5'3"*). If you are lengthier, expect to be cramped with less legroom than most Southwest and Spirit flights.

Depending on your location and time of day, the buses are susceptible to overcrowding and standing may be your only option. Women and the elderly get priority seating. If you see one standing, it is proper to give up your seat.

Standing can be inconvenient if your bus outing was to the grocery store. Leaning in the aisle with your groceries in tow is difficult but not impossible. Overcrowding only occurs in the busier cities and usually only during rush hour. Ecuadorians are comfortable in tight quarters unlike most North Americans, so don't

expect them to try to keep to their space if it's cramped.

If you board hungry or thirsty, not to worry, venders often hop aboard and offer sweet and salty snacks or beverages for under a dollar.

Most local buses cost $0.25 and arrive within minutes of their schedule Ecuador Bus Schedule[5]

Take care of your belongings while on the bus. Although I have not seen or experienced any trouble, I have read cautions and have heard of people who donated their bags in the overhead compartments to a quick moving local. Keep your belongings on your lap and/or in-between your legs.

OWNING A VEHICLE

I've always preferred the freedom having a set of wheels provides, however, there are special considerations while living abroad. There are a few extra hoops to jump through when owning a vehicle in Ecuador. After you successfully purchase a car, knowing what

---

[5] http://www.ecuadorschedules.com/

to do if it breaks down is an entirely different story. Communicating with a mechanic in Spanish, taking care of preventative maintenance, and renewing the registration are all different beasts in Ecuador. See *Buying a Car* in the ***Once You Have Arrived*** section for more information.

TAXIS

Taxis are available and affordable across the country. Make sure and only hire licensed cabs by calling a service, hiring a cab from the licensed stands (in the airport), or asking a restaurant or business owner to call one for you.

DRIVING IN ECUADOR

Ecuador has an excellent infrastructure. The roads are fairly well marked along the coast and most large cities, and are easy to locate on your GPS device. That being said, not all GPS devices are created equal! I had a friend whose GPS worked fine heading north in Ecuador but failed to work heading south! Once off the beaten path, however, highways may not have signage. Driving at night can be particularly hazardous as many mountain roads are damaged by heavy rains or are obstructed by heavy fog. The latter occurs most frequently in the afternoon and night.

Taking the wheel is not for the faint of heart. In one outing you may be required to navigate around tractors, horses, cows, and other speedy drivers. You will frequently witness drivers cross into oncoming traffic to pass slow vehicles. In my recent past, I worked as a paramedic and often drove the ambulance with lights and sirens. Driving in much of Latin America is just like that but without the lights and sirens offering a warning, because after all, it's the status quo.

Many residents opt out of driving at night because of the increase in difficulty, danger, and lack of lighting. With the Ecuadorian pace and based on your personality, that choice might not even cause an inconvenience.

Thankfully, there is not the same issue of officers pulling gringos over for a bribe like in other Latin American countries. Amy Prisco, an expat for over nine years, said that she has never been pulled over for a violation although she has been asked to have her car checked along with every other car at stop-points four times over the nine years without incidence.

I have happily utilized the Google Maps App on my iPhone for my navigational needs. Cellular service and an unlocked phone are required. Read more about cellular services in the **Once You Have Arrived** section.

IDENTIFICATION

It is highly recommended that you carry a copy of your passport and valid stamp on your person at all times until you receive your residency card or *cedula*. It doesn't sound practical but it's required. Thankfully, expats before us have mastered the process.

There are numerous stores that offer *"copias"* or copies and lamination services. They can create a copy of your passport picture and shrink it to a standard card size. Then they copy the most recent entrance stamp on the back of the card. Finally, they laminate the card, giving you a plastic waterproof card that is portable and easy to carry in your board shorts or wallet. If you are pulled over without this ID, you could find yourself in some trouble.

IMMIGRATION

MANY ARE THE PATHS TO ECUADOR. THIS SECTION COVERS THE MOST COMMON
IMMIGRATION ROUTES TO AN ECUADORIAN LIFE

Ecuador is no longer a secret. International Living gave it the blue ribbon on their 2014 Annual Global Retirement Index, calling it "The World's Best Haven!" Ecuador grabbed the number two slot for best place to retire by Forbes (Panama captured number one by 1/10th a point). The international community is flocking towards the middle of the world for good reason.

The climate is luxurious, the pace relaxed, the cost of living is cheap, nature abounds, and you can live at most any altitude you desire.

However, Ecuador is just like other Latin American countries when it comes to paperwork. They love their paperwork completed with all the i's dotted and t's crossed. That being said, if you have perfect paperwork, you can have your residency card, *cedula,* in your hot little hands in under 30 days! I know someone who received their visa in only two weeks. This efficiency is almost unheard of in Latin America, so don't take it for granted! To provide you with some perspective, Costa Rica can take multiple years even though the government reports a six month wait.

Now this is not the case for everyone. I know some people in Ecuador with nightmare multiple year immigration experiences. Because of this, I really recommend that you solicit help from someone who has years of experience and can provide numerous glowing reviews. See the *Services* section for companies where I interviewed a representative and their customers.

THE ABC's OF RESIDENCY

Below are the most popular routes to your cedula or residency card.

- Pensioner Visa 9-I
- Investor Visa 9-II
- Industrial Investor Visa 9-III
- Agent Visa 9-IV
- Professional Visa 9-V
- Dependent Visa 9-VI

RESIDENCY 101+

Immigration can be a very complex topic which is why I advise you to get help. Whether you use a visa specialist *(sometimes an expat that has helped so many people obtain residency they have become a visa guru)* or a lawyer, make sure you check their references. Some people spend a few grand without checking out the person or service and the attorney doesn't do a damn thing for them.

That being said, self-education is a great way to

save time and learn the right questions to ask.

This section dives deeper into each category including requirements, paperwork, and stipulations. If you're a "not into the details" kinda' person and would rather leave that up to the pros, then go ahead and skip forward to the next chapter.

The immigration process usually includes three steps: securing your visa, censo (Ecuadorian ID required only of foreigners), and cedula (ID card required of ALL Ecuadorians).

Pensioner Visa 9-I

To apply as a pensioner, you must prove that you have a stable monthly income of at least $800 for yourself, and an additional $100 per dependent. This stable income is usually in the form of a social security check, annuity, pension, or trust.

EXPAT EXPERIENCE

"I went through office moves, law changes, etc. getting my papers straightened out. It took me 22 trips and a lot of money, but I finally did get it all sorted out and became a legal resident for the 2nd time."
~ Connie Wilson, expat from Houston

Connie's husband passed and because her cedula was acquired as a dependent, she had to secure her paperwork again during a very sad and stressful time. In order to avoid this, if you qualify and apply as individuals instead of a family for your visas, censos, and cedulas, you will pay more up front but is considered by many worth the money in order to avoid the hassles of Ecuadorian immigration.

Dom Buonamici has a popular email newsletter where he shares his experiences of how to live and invest in Ecuador. He wrote the following article about how he helped some folks get their visas in Ecuador in just 4 hours and a 2 week wait for the visas themselves to be ready:

1. Bring down the following documents from the USA, their home country...
- Proof of pension
- Marriage certificate

- Birth certificates (just in case, although lately they are no longer asking for these)
- Criminal record check from where they've lived the last 5 years (the document itself can be no older than 6 months) ** This is not accurate, they have changed this requirement to requiring an FBI report, instead of your local police criminal record.**
- Certificate from the Ecuador consulate in your home country certifying the source of pension document. (Certificado determinando la percepción de dicha jubilación, pensión) This is a new one since I helped someone with this last year!

All the above documents need to be apostilled by the Secretary of State in the State they are issued, and the proof of pension needs to be certified by the nearest Ecuador Consulate before coming.

2. Then, we went straight to the Immigration police (in Manta it's the Immigration office on 4 de Noviembre, in Quito its the immigration office across from the Mall El Jardin) to get a document for each showing all their migratory movements in and out of Ecuador called the Certificado de Movimiento Migratorio. (cost $5 each) Elapsed time 20 minutes.

3. Then, we made color copies of the info page of both their passports and of the page showing their latest stamp upon entry to Ecuador. We also had passport photos taken of each. And then we printed off the official visa application form found here so each person could fill one in. I also bought a manilla folder to put all their documents. Elapsed time 15 minutes.

4. Then I translated the documents they brought from the States and went to a local notary next to the Pichincha Bank in the center of Manta where I had to verify my signature as the document translator and get something called a RECONOCIMIENTO DE FIRMA. ($20). Anyone can translate the documents except the interested party. Elapsed time 1 hour 45 minutes.

5. Then in an internet cafe across the street from the bus terminal in the center of Manta, I wrote up in Spanish a simple letter stating to the immigration department what they want to do (retire in Ecuador) and why they want to retire here (I said the weather). Elapsed time 10 minutes.

6. Went with all the documents and my friends who were applying (they have to be present or you need to have a power of attorney document notarized) to the Ministerio de Relaciones Exteriores in the center of town inbetween the boardwalk area (Malecon) and the big Pichincha Bank. We got a turn and there was no wait so we turned in the folder with all the above. They also had to pay the application fee of $30 each. Elapsed time 20 minutes.

In two weeks they'll have to go back to that same office once their visas are approved, pay the visa fee at the window ($320 each, one time only) and then they will place the visas in the passports and give you 30 days to get a cedula which is your official Ecuadorian ID card (which as of June 2014 you cannot do in Manta, only Quito, Guayaquil or Cuenca).

Then they will be permanent Ecuador residents who can stay in country as long as they like.

Not bad for 4 hours.

~ Dom Buonamici, Quito Airport Suites

Investor Visa 9-II

To qualify for the Investor visa, you need to throw some cash into the game to the tune of $25,000 USD, at either a property, CD (certificate of deposits), or government bonds. Throw in an additional $500 to qualify each dependent for residency. With this method, however, if a lien is added to the home or you sell the property, it results in the loss of your residency.

If bonds or CDs are purchased, those investments cannot be liquified as long as the applicant wishes to maintain his/her residency. You can, however, withdraw the interest accrued. This option is only for those who have a nest egg they don't plan on using for sometime, or for those who plan on purchasing a property.

Industrial Investor Visa 9-III

This route is for trade investors looking to export products from an industrial, agricultural, international, or livestock arena. It requires a large chunk of change, starting at $30,000.

Agent Visa 9-IV

Those who intend to work permanently for a legally established company in Ecuador apply for this visa. They usually perform technical or specialized skills that satisfy a need that is lacking in the Ecuadorian talent pool. This visa can also satisfy the requirements for members of religious organizations, or those who open a legal Ecuadorian business and hire at least 80% Ecuadorian personnel.

Professional Visa 9-V

This visa is proof that what your parents told you about getting your bachelors degree is right, it does make a difference! You can obtain a professional bias by presenting a degree recognized by a national university.[6] In addition to your degree, you must bring your professional title, credentials, and transcripts to be evaluated and validated by an Ecuadorian University after they've been apostilled by the Secretary of State in the US (if that's where your school is located). If your profession doesn't exist in Ecuador, the degree must be locally certified. Also, if there's a specific Ecuadorian requirement such as a medical board exam or bar exam, the applicant needs to satisfy said requirements.

Dependent Visa 9-VI

This visa is for those who are blood relatives: spouse, children, parent, grandparent, or sibling of a *resident* or citizen. They simply need to provide paperwork proving their relation to the previously mentioned person.

IMMIGRATION WITH CHILDREN

Due to an increase in juvenile sex trafficking, Ecuador has placed a special exit requirement for minors in an effort to battle this acknowledged problem. Citizens and residents of Ecuador, under the age of 18 who are traveling alone, with one parent, or a third party must carry a copy of their birth certificate and a written consent from the non-present parent(s) or legal guardian. If a parent is deceased, a notarized copy of their death certificate must be presented.

WHERE DO YOU START?

Whether or not you opt to use a service, the starting point of the process is procuring documents from your home country. Dr. Chiluisa, an expat attorney stated, *"It's very rare for an expat to arrive with all of their documents, this is partly due*

---

[6] SNIESE (Sistema nacional de Información de la Educación Superior del Ecuador) compiled a list of acceptable universities.

to the fact the rules are in constant flux, and because there is a lot of misinformation out there."

Luckily, if you forget a few documents or learn of changes after you arrive to Ecuador, there are services like EcuaAssist that can secure all of your documents for you through their partner offices in California and the FBI criminal records in Washington D.C. That being said, do your best to bring your documents yourself because if you don't, it will significantly delay your immigration process (4 -5 months instead of 5 - 6 weeks).

Below are some basic documents to get started on:

☐ Make sure that your passport is not near its expiration! It must have at least six months left upon application and empty pages available

☐ A good girl/boy FBI criminal record (As of Jan 2014 your criminal background must come from the FBI instead of your local police department)

☐ Medical certificate

☐ Two notarized copies of an up-to-date passport with the notary attesting to the fact that the status is legally current

☐ A completed form *"hoja de datos para la cédula"* (a data card)

☐ Two passport-size photos in color with a white backdrop

Each visa will require a variety of supporting documents that often need to be authenticated by the Ecuadorian Consul.

Special Considerations

★ Once you secure residency, you're not permitted to leave the country for longer than 90 days your first two years. After your rookie years are complete, the rule loosens to: not staying out of country for more than 18 consecutive months in order to retain your residency.

★All of the documents obtained in the United States MUST be originals and notarized by a local notary if they do not have a government seal.

★All documents must be authenticated by the Ecuadorian Consul.

★Each document must be legally translated into Spanish.

★After all of your documents have been prepared, translated, notarized, and authenticated... phew... Then, fork over another $350 for the application fee (unless you are disabled)[7] and sit back and relax for the short 30 day wait.

★Your immigration agent can legally ask you to provide any other legal document they find necessary for your immigration process. This means no two immigration procedures are necessarily equal.

★During the waiting period, you are permitted to stay in the country until a decision has been granted. You can also leave the country and return if so desired. You will be provided a docket number to display to immigration officials that show you are in the process of becoming a resident.

TIP
Ecuador LOVES paperwork and stamps, so just get used to it. Everything has a process, and theirs involves lots of trees. You may be adapted to an electronic era, just remember that era does not exist *yet* in Ecuador.

At the end of the paperwork, you can live here: Along Ruta del Sol, near Salinas.

---

[7] As of May 2014, persons that are verified disabled by the Ecuadorian government do not have to pay the application fee for residency.

EXPAT EXPERIENCE

"We went to Guayaquil on Tuesday and got our censo cards. The same morning we went to the Civil Register office to get our cedulas done, BUT the computer wouldn't accept our birthplace as New Mexico. We had to go back to immigration and have our form changed to show the birth county, and they would not do that without a copy of the birth certificates. We did not have our birth certificates with us. While they have copies of them in that same building, we had to come back to Salinas to get our birth certificates, and return to Guayaquil on Wednesday. After several hours they FINALLY got the computer to accept the counties."
~ Connie Wilson, expat since 2011

To learn more about Immigration and legal services, see *How to File For Residency* in the **After You Have Arrived** section.

Congratulations! You have figured out how you can legally live in one of the top rated retirement havens on earth! Now, where to land?

PART II

Where is Your Haven?

HELPING YOU DISCOVER WHERE IN ECUADOR IS YOUR SWEET SPOT

WHERE IN Ecuador IS YOUR HAVEN?

FINDING YOUR SLICE OF HEAVEN IS ALL ABOUT WASP

Deciding where to live in your home country can be daunting, but in a foreign country, it can be downright overwhelming! Not to worry, however, because a long line of expats have *lived and learned* and will pave your way with their lessons in the following pages. Let us save you from the mistakes that we've made.

Where you decide to settle in Ecuador can make or break your experience. I've developed an acronym to help guide your *must haves* and *wants* to reach the location that best fits your needs: **W.A.S.P.**- Weather, Activities/Amenities, Social requirements, and Proximity to airport.

WEATHER

As mentioned in the *Basics* section, Ecuador has a variety

of excellent climate options. In addition to an array of climates, because the country is located on the equator, the sun pours down for twelve hours each day! Your region may or may not have clouds impeding the sun some of those hours.

If you like it tropical, hot and humid, head to the coast. If you enjoy cool mornings, warm afternoons, and sleeping with a blanket or two at night, then the Sierra region would be a good fit! If spring weather sends you to your happy place, then Cuenca could suit you well.

Keep in mind that if mountain towns such as Quito or Cuenca are too cold, and coastal cities such as Salinas or Montañita are too hot, there are other options. In a country with towns across hundreds of different elevations, your temperature sweet-spot could be just up or down the mountain. For example, instead of Cuenca, try out nearby Gualaceo, Paute, or Yunguilla Valley. They are all located at lower elevations

making them a bit warmer but not hot. Or if you'd like to live within reach of Quito, but it's also too cold, try nearby towns Tumbaco or Los Chillos.

To see detailed weather reports of each region in Ecuador visit: http://bit.ly/ECweather

EXPAT EXPERIENCE

"The number one factor for where I wanted to live was the weather. I have froze most my life. I'm from the northeast and James is from Scandinavia.

We went to Quito and Otavalo, and found them to be too cold at night. James had altitude sickness and difficulty breathing with his heart problem. So we headed to the coast. In very little time he was breathing better and we were thriving. It is a bit too hot in Feb/Mar but is worth the trade off."
~ Bev Petersen, expat from Wisconsin

ACTIVITIES

What *activities* would you like to access on a regular basis? Do you enjoy hiking, soaking in hot springs, exploring caves, strolling along expansive beaches, peering into volcanos, bathing in waterfalls, or fishing in streams? Are you a birder? Do you plan to keep your mind active with hobbies, part time work, volunteering in your community, or social endeavors?

Do you imagine yourself amongst the clouds in the cloud forest, along an expansive coconut palmed lined beach, near crater lakes that you can kayak through, deep in the forest or jungles, living amongst the Andes, in a birder's haven, near a lake or rivers where you can fly-fish, kayak or white-water raft? Do you want to live in or near a Quechan community?

Make sure to research your area so it satisfies these desires. A life lounging by the pool becomes devoid of purpose after the initial high of the first few months wears off.

Young adults without kids looking for a place to meet like-minded people tend to be dissatisfied if they buy a house in an isolated jungle in Ecuador's amazon! The isolation could drive you mad!

If you seek *night life* and *social events,* make sure your location can deliver. If your idea of perfection is a relaxing path less traveled, don't opt for hot spots like Montañita and Guayaquil.

AMENITIES

This section is dedicated to lifestyle. Do you want an American-styled home or an Ecuadorian-styled home? Are you looking for granite, stainless steel, cable internet, air conditioning, etc? Or are you hoping for a small home with an outdoor kitchen, wood construction, packed with charm and a modest price tag?

No two places are created equal, therefore each location has its trade offs. You need to create a "must have" list, and stick to it! Are you looking for an urban area, a suburb, a place off-the-grid, or somewhere in-between? Keep in mind that houses located along thick jungles or in isolated mountain pueblos may not have internet. They might not even have city water. Decide what your deal breakers are and stick to them! Do you require cable internet or would a 3g stick[8] work for you? Do you need to live in a place where electricity rarely fails and where the water supply is consistent? Or are you a candle toting adventurer willing to get away from it all including electricity from time to time to delve deeper into untouched beauty?

Another amenity to consider is medical facilities. If you have a long history of cardiac, diabetic, cancer, or other speciality illness then you should really add this to your list of considerations. Most speciality hospitals are located in Cuenca, Quito, and Guayaquil.

SOCIAL REQUIREMENTS

Whether you're stag, hitched, or family-toting, you need to decide what types of social interaction you would like close by. Are you hoping to volunteer in your community? Do you seek a healthy expat presence in your neighborhood to exchange stories and solicit support from? Cuenca, Lojas, Salinas, and Cotacachi all have healthy expat communities.

A lush getaway in the jungle may be exotic and romantic, but if you are an extravert and your only neighbors are the four-legged variety, this could lead to problems.

PROXIMITY TO AIRPORT

How often do you plan on visiting folks at home? How often do you wish to host family and friends in Ecuador? Your proximity to the airport can play a huge part in how difficult it is to accomplish these goals. How far is too far? Do you find it exciting to live down a 3 hour dirt road? Be advised, Google Maps may serve well for driving directions, but it fails miserably with time estimation. Talk to a local or

---

[8] A 3G stick is a USB device that provides a much slower and less reliable internet connection based on a cellular plan to which you subscribe

look at a bus schedule for best estimates.

A two hour commute in Ecuador can be much more taxing than a two hour commute in North America. It's hard to explain, but something about the combination of smaller roads, navigating around numerous painfully slow 18-wheelers and tractors, decreased signage and familiarity, and a different driving culture all combine into an exhaustive driving experience.

TO SUM UP

Now that you have a grasp on *WHAT* you want, let's walk through *WHERE* in Ecuador offers your perfect combination of wants and needs.

Ecuador has twenty-four providences that are scattered across four main regions: *the Coast, the Galápagos Islands, the Sierra, and Amazonia (or Oriente)*.

THE COAST

◆Population: 7,206,500
◆Most populated region
◆ Guayaquil International
Airport

◆Fisheries
◆Gateway to the Galápagos
Islands

Ecuador's population was concentrated in the mountains until the 19th century when the coast's chronic malaria and yellow fever problems subsided. Now, the coastal region is Ecuador's most fertile zone. Large exports such as bananas and rice are grown here. There are also numerous active fisheries along the coast.

The region begins just west of the Andean range and contains: Esmeraldas, Guayas, Los Ríos, Manabí, El Oro, and Santa Elena provinces. The largest city in the coastal region by a long shot is Guayaquil. In fact, it's the most populated city in Ecuador!

Along the coast you can find a variety of towns. Sleepy fishing villages such as Anconcito, up and coming beach towns like Ballena, urban beach towns filled with high-rises like Salinas, and Guayaquil, a city filled with hustle and bustle. Tropical heat is something they all have in common. If you want to escape the heat, escape the beach.

Esmeraldas - *population 534,000*

This is Ecuador's most northern coastal region and most culturally diverse town. Esmeraldas is where cultures from around the world collide amidst jungle, river, and ocean. Until a few decades ago, it was only accessible by boat. Due to the isolation, the Tumaco/ La Tolita cultures were the only inhabitants for centuries.

The slaves that escaped the working sugarcane fields to the North re-located to this border region. They created the "Republic of Blacks," a haven for escaping slaves in South America. Over time their culture intertwined with the indigenous people creating a vibrant melting pot.

Once the port, roads, cruise liners, and the Trans-Ecuador pipeline entered the scene, Esmeraldas became a commercial zone filled with dismal concrete buildings. It is a distinct contrast to the laid back beach towns only minutes away. There have been many reports of Colombia's trouble spilling into this region of Ecuador. We are seeing increased crime, drug trafficking, a few instances of kidnapping, and other criminal activity.

On the flip side, the natural assets just minutes outside of the commercial zone are seemingly endless. If you enjoy canoeing or kayaking, the wild and remote inlets make for an amazing backyard experience.

Guayas - *population 3,645,145*

This province is home to the most populated city in Ecuador, Guayaquil.

Guayaquil

Guayaquil is a town filled with taxis, hotels, malls, restaurants, marinas, and more! It's a port town and the largest city in Ecuador. That's a double whammy with regard to crime which is why Guayaquil is not for the faint of heart. See the *Crime* section in *Basics* for more information.

The business atmosphere is more relaxed, and meetings will never begin on schedule.

There is a lovely Malecón you can walk along, but keep a mindful eye out. A leisurely stroll during the day can turn into a very bad situation at night.

EXPAT QUOTE

If you were to arrive in EC today, where would you live?
"I'm a city girl. I might give Guayaquil a shot. It's not an easy city to like, but over time it grows on you. The people are direct, like New Yorkers, and their temperaments can run hot – just like the weather. The line between politeness and hypocrisy is sometimes a vague one. They are movers and shakers and mean business, but sure know how to relax and kick back."
~ Amy Prisco
Expat from New York since 2006
alprisco@gmail.com

Montañita

Pachouli wearing, dreadlocks toting, Mary Jane enthusiasts dig Montañita. It's a small town famous for surfing and the laid-back hippie vibe it exudes. Life is not completely chill, however, because the little beach town can really get cranking at night. It isn't unusual to see roaring beach parties complete with fire throwers. If you are an early to bed type and want to make Montañita your home, make sure to live far enough away from the clubs.

Los Ríos - *population 778,178*

This province earns its keep through the production of: coffee, cacao, bananas, and rice. Recently, it has dipped its toes into tourism by enticing tourists to take fishing tours and observe native rituals.

The region is mostly flat with the highest hills measuring in at 500 feet. The rivers feed into the beauty of the region and sustain the fertile lands. December through June (winter) sees a substantial amount of rainfall. The rest of the year is fairly dry and warm with an average temperature of 77 degrees F (25 degrees C).

Manabí - *population 1,339,025*

This Central Pacific province is known for its fishing villages, Machalilla National Park, rich biodiversity, and is the commercial center of Manta. Its infrastructure is sound, and public transportation is easy to navigate. The seafood here is remarkable! Up and coming expat towns: Puerto Lopez and Puerto Cayo are located in this province.

Manta

Manta is located in Manabí province and is home to the second largest port in Ecuador. It's a major commercial, holiday, and expat hotspot which is why the nights host hordes of partying people, loud music, and meandering cars. It's a common weekend getaway location, so you can expect more crowds on Saturday and Sunday, especially during a holiday.

EXPAT QUOTE

"Mark and I love Puerto Cayo because of the small town feel. There are no condo buildings blocking the views and the beach is empty almost all year. It's not a huge tourist destination, so most of the people we either know by sight or they know of us."
~ Diane & Mark Bublack, expats from Houston

El Oro - *population 600,540*

El Oro translates to *gold* and was named after its rich gold mining history. Today it's rich in water filled with mangroves, rivers, marshes, and canals. The western portion of the province is lower lying and is subjected to occasional flooding. The eastern portion is scattered with mountains.

Near the Peruvian border you will find the Islands of Jambeli, an oasis that has been converted into a tourist attraction thanks to easy boat access from Puerto Bolivar.

The climate is relatively dry and warm, averaging 73 degrees F (23 degrees C).

Santa Elena - *population 308,889*

The most popular expat town in Santa Elena is beachfront Salinas.

Salinas

Here you will find high rise luxury condos and a gorgeous topaz ocean. There are numerous restaurants along the malecón (boardwalk), or if you prefer to stay on your rented chaise lounger, feel free to buy nourishment from the food and drink venders that troll the beach. The weekends bring in a hoard of Ecuadorians looking to let loose after a long work week. There are seasonal events where a full scale stage is set up in the sand and they party into the wee hours of the night. The downside to this is after the weekend warriors depart, they leave a trail of trash behind.

Taxis are plentiful and cheap. One dollar gets you anywhere along the main strip. There are countless places to eat including Sushi and Italian!

Hundreds of expats decide to plant in Santa Elena, and many decide to contribute to local causes such as Expats Helping Kids in Ecuador.

The coast doesn't have a Gringo Tree but beach-loving expats are in the process of starting their own newsletter.[9]

---

[9] http://bit.ly/salinasnewsletter

La Libertad[10]

Also located in Santa Elena is this authentic Ecuadorian town. You can buy just about anything you need here. I'm not talking name brands and fancy malls, instead there are endless craft, gift, electronic, and miscellaneous stores selling anything you can dream up. My wife bought material for her wedding dress here.

There is also excellent local food options. Countless street venders walk around wheeling their food down the street in a wheelbarrow carrying a trash can that has a working fire inside.

While there is not a huge expat following here and Spanish skills are required, this is a great authentic coastal town only 10 minutes from expat hotspot, Salinas.

---

[10] Watch a video that provides a sneak preview into La Libertad: http://bit.ly/Libertadvid

THE GALÁPAGOS ISLANDS

- Population: 25,124
- Seymour Airport, Baltra Island
- No indigenous population EVER
- 5 islands are inhabited
- $100 entry fee

The Galápagos Islands (official name: Archipiélago de Colón) are filled with nature's secrets. It was these islands that helped provide answers to how nature functions. Darwin studied the birds of the islands that existed nowhere else on earth. In 1859, after years of research, he wrote his conclusions in *On the Origin of Species*.

Another fun fact is that the Gálapagos Islands are one of the few places in the world that doesn't have an indigenous population. I don't think it's a coincidence that the fundamental aspect of nature's progression was discovered where people didn't exist. Humans migrated to the islands only in the last century and most from mainland Ecuador. Even a hundred years after Darwin's *On the Origin of Species,* there were only 1000 - 2000 residents. A census conducted in 2010 reveals just over 25,000 people living on the islands.

Tourism is the main fiscal purpose of the islands. However, Ecuador understands how important nature is there and has imposed many regulations in an attempt to keep the Galápagos clean.

◆There is a second bag check (by hand) required on all flights headed to the Galápagos. After the additional bag check is completed, your bag is zip-tied with a special tag, so the attendants can see if you have accessed your bag.

◆In route to the islands, the flight attendants open all overhead compartments and spray a disinfectant/bug killer to assure that our bags do not inadvertently import any germs or insects.

◆Most tourism traffic is concentrated in Santa Cruz. That's where the hotels, restaurants, and tourism kiosks are based. The adjoined island Baltra is home to the newly renovated international airport.

◆A certified nature guide is required to venture to the outer island to assure the safety of all nature and wildlife.

◆If you bring a bag on an excursion to an outer island, it will be searched once you arrive to guarantee you aren't bringing in anything that could hurt the animals.

Each island is unique with varying species, altitudes, and rainfall. Because of cooler water currents, rain occurs year-round in the Galápagos. June through November, however, offers some relief to the heat, averaging 72 degrees F (22 C) along the coast with frequent drizzles and fog. Not a great time to visit as a tourist since visibility is down and waves are up. December through May is filled with sunshine, 80 degree F weather, and fewer showers.

Out of the eighteen main islands, only five of them are inhabited: Baltra, Floreana, Isabela, San Cristobal and Santa Cruz.

The second largest island, Santa Cruz, is where everything happens! More specifically, Puerto Ayora is where it's all at! Santa Cruz Island is a dormant volcano that is believed to have last erupted over a million years ago. There is an enormous lava tunnel over 2000 meters (6562 feet) long that you can walk through. The volcano left reminders of its activity in the form of two big holes formed when a magma chamber collapsed, now referred to as Los Gemelos or "The Twins." You can hike around the Twins with a short bus ride on the way out of Puerto Ayora.

More sea lions walk the streets and live in the boats docked in Puerto Ayora than people. Each time I passed a sea lion in the road, I mistook it for a statue, then it would move and startle me. I found one sea lion lounging poolside at a nice water-front hotel. If he could speak, I'm pretty sure he would have ordered a foo-foo drink with an umbrella in it.

Santa Cruz Island is a pretty special place where the animals thrive and are protected and respected. Just from the docks at Puerto Ayora I saw: blue heron, egrets, black tipped reef shark, thousands of pelicans, colorful crabs, marine iguanas, sea lions, hundreds of manta rays, and two sea turtles!

If you are hoping to find a job working at a restaurant, hotel, or tour operator, or even start your own business, this would be the best island for you.

Baltra Island

The island was established as a United States Air Force base during World War II. This location helped to spot enemy submarines.

This dry and desolate island is filled with salt bushes and prickly pear cactus. Don't be surprised when this is your first taste of the famed Galápagos Islands! You will land in the brand new airport (finished construction in early 2014) that is promoted as "the first ecological airport worldwide." After landing, a bus will herd you to the nearby docks where a boat taxi will take you the five - ten minute journey to Santa Cruz. Make sure and have a few dollars in small change for the boat operator as they can't break large bills.

Floreana Island

Isla Floreana was named after Juan José Flores, the first president of Ecuador. It was during his administration that the government took possession of Galápagos. This island was also formed by a volcanic eruption.

Floreana[11] is a popular tour, snorkeling, and diving destination. A favorite dive and snorkel site, "Devil's Crown," is located just off the northeast point of the island. There you can swim along an underwater volcanic cone with schools of fish, sea turtles, sharks and sea lions! After you dry off, the tour usually heads up the hill

---

[11] Watch a two minute video of an Isla Floreana tour here: http://bit.ly/floreannatour

where you can observe the great tortoises and the Galápagos finch, a bird that only exits in one region of Isla Floreana and nowhere else on earth!

The island was once more lively in ways of vegetation and animal species, however, an idiotic helmsman, Thomas Chappel of the whaling ship Essex, decided it would be funny to light a small fire while hunting on Charles Island. Since it was the height of the dry season, the fire raged out of control in seconds and forced Tom and the other hunters to run through the flames in order to escape.

By the time the hunters made it back to the Essex, almost the entire island was burning. Captain Pollard was infuriated and swore vengeance on whoever had set the fire. Chappel didn't fess up for some time. After a full day of sailing, the fire was still visible on the horizon. Idiotic Tom burned the entire island down without consequence.

Karmically, the ship of said whaler was sunk by a massive

bull sperm whale one year later.

Isabela Island

The largest of the Galápagos Islands was named in honor of Queen Isabela. Fun fact: It is the only island to have the equator run across it! Ok, one more: It is also the only place in the world where a penguin can be in its natural habitat in the *Northern* Hemisphere.

The island is shaped much like a seahorse due to six large volcanoes converging into a single land mass. The island is home to many lovely critters including: Galápagos penguins, flightless cormorants, marine iguanas, pelicans, sally lightfoot crabs, land iguanas, Galápagos tortoises, Darwin finches, Galápagos hawks, and Galápagos doves.

Even though it earns the gold medallion for land mass, it only secures the bronze for population. The third-largest human settlement of the Archipelago, Puerto Villamil, is located at the southeastern tip of the island.

San Cristobal

One of the oldest islands in the Archipelago recently opened an airport enabling you to fly direct from Guayaquil! Puerto Baquerizo Moreno, the capital of the Archipelago, is located on the southwestern tip of the island and is home to the second largest population in the Galápagos, 5,600 (mostly fishermen). It's the most eastern island in the Archipelago and is home to: frigate birds, sea lions, tortoises, blue and red footed boobies, marine iguanas, and dolphins.

Tourism and fishing are the primary means of income on the island. The tourism network is not as advanced as Puerto Ayora but is up-and-coming!

The largest fresh water lake in the Archipelago, *Laguna El Junco,* is located in the crater of San Cristóbal.

Healthcare Services Available

If you are considering a move to the islands, pay special attention to the medical services there. If you are young and healthy, the risk may not be much of a hurdle, but if you have health problems or concerns then this could pose a problem. Puerto Ayora has a "hospital" that is poorly stocked and can only handle minor problems. Surgeries are not performed there. The hospital is located on Av. Padre J. Herrera.

Puerto Baquerizo Moreno also has a poorly equipped hospital called Oskar Jandi, located at Av. Northia y Av. Quito (across from Hotel Mar Azul). It operates more like an urgent care than a hospital. However, times are a' changing! The United States donated an impressive $8.1 million dollar investment towards construction of a new hospital in Puerto Baquerizo Moreno. In addition to the new facility, there is a Navy operated Bell-430 helicopter dedicated to emergency evacuations and medical transfers.

THE SIERRA

◆Population: 5,038,100
◆UNESCO World Heritage cities Quito & Cuenca
◆Quito airport
◆Heavy indigenous influences
◆Mild temperatures

In the Sierra, you can admire snow-capped mountains, flirt with active volcanos, stroll through a charm-filled UNESCO world heritage city, and observe an older way of life in Cotacachi.

The region's main agricultural focuses are on potato, maize (corn), and quinoa.

The Sierra includes provinces: Azuay, Cañar, Carchi, Chimborazo, Imbabura, Loja, Pichincha, and Tungurahua.

Azuay - *population 600,000*

While Azuay doesn't have high mountains to impress with, the northern region of Cajas can still take your breath away. The 300 lagoons and massive condors taking flight are enough to tickle any nature lover's fancy. Plus, a few mighty rivers slice through the province connecting the region to the Amazon.

Azuay is home to the largest Ecuadorian expat hub, *Cuenca,* which might contribute to the fact that it holds Ecuador's highest growth rate. If the growth rate remains unchanged, the population of the urban area will double in fifteen years!

Cuenca

Cuenca exists at the convergence of four rivers and is surrounded by mountains on every side covered in grass or trees. In addition to a wealth of natural assets, it's filled with beautiful architecture and parks. There are several universities in the area, adding some additional flare. There are also three major hospitals that provide top standards of care. While their hospitals are up to date to international standards, their merchants are not. Most places in Cuenca only accept cash, so make sure and plan ahead.

Cuenca is not only a huge expat hub, it too is a UNESCO World Heritage Trust site. Of the 600,000 people in the province, about 500,000 of them reside in the Cuenca Canton (similar to a county).

Common complaints from expats living in Cuenca are poor air quality (due to emission of large buses on narrow streets) and too much rain and clouds. Cuenca is often called the "land of eternal springtime." Alongside those spring showers are ideal temperatures for many: 60s to 70s during the day (15 - 21 C). It can get chilly at night at its elevation of 8,400 feet (2560 m) and averages 40s to 50s (4 - 10 C). Important to note, there aren't heaters in even the most modern buildings in Cuenca, so blankets and sweaters are a must in the evenings and mornings.

April is by far the wettest month, nicknamed the month of "a thousand rains *(mil aguas)*. On average, Cuenca sees no fewer than 10 days of rain per month and no greater than 22.[12]

Cañar - *population 225,981*

Cañar is best known for the Temple of the Sun, located in Ecuador's most famous Inca settlement, Ingapirca. The mood at these ruins is almost palpable. It is something that everyone visiting or living in Ecuador should experience. The town was named after its indigenous people, the Cañari, whose brave fierceness allowed them to maintain much of their culture in spite of Spanish pressures.

In addition to the ruins, Cañar is home to the stunning landscapes of San Luis and the authentic small town of Biblian. Both towns are esthetically wrapped in green hills.

This province is an excellent base for hiking and mountain biking enthusiasts. There are a variety of treks that take you through the ruins and to the undisturbed lakes in the region. In fact, many argue that hiking the region is the best way to experience it!

Carchi - *population 164,939*

Carchi is nicknamed *heir of the sun and earth* for a reason. Here you can sooth your body in the thermal baths in Aguas Hedionas or Calera, swim under de Paluz Falls (a waterfall located in San Gabriel), or hike through El Angel Ecological Reserve! Lagunas Verdes, three lakes filled with sulphur rich blue-green water, is a great stopping point between Tufiño and Maldonado.

This province is not all paradise, however, since it spans to the Colombian border. Like any border town, Tulcán is popping with people and products traveling every which way! The border crossing here is unique. A seven kilometer (4.3 mile) international stone-bridge created by the Incas and named Rumichaca, is shared by the two countries.

---

[12] A day of rain is qualified by at least .1mm of measurable rainfall

In addition to commercial madness, the town managed to create a three acre topiary garden cemetery that is recognized as the most elaborate topiary in the New World.

Chimborazo - *population 458,632*

This province is hilly and home to Ecuador's highest peak. The glacier summit of Chimborazo Volcano measures 20,564 feet high(6268 meters)! There are several lakes in the area due to the increase of glacier melt. The primary lakes include: Colta, Colay Cocha, and Ozogoche. The cities that reside along the nooks and crannies of this province are usually cooler to live in than most expats enjoy. However, this province provides picture perfect day trips to Sangay National Park and Chimborazo Volcano.

Chimborazo is not the highest peak in the world, but it still snatches the title of *summit furthest from the Earth's center!* This is because the earth is not perfectly circular, it is fattest across the equator. So, while Mount Everest is higher in perspective to the sea level, Chimborazo, which is located only 1 degree away from the equator, is considered the furthest peak from the center of the Earth. This handy fact places Chimborazo on thousands of elite hiker's bucket list. The best time to climb this ice-ridden beast is December through January and July through August.

While the volcano is currently inactive, the last eruption is believed to have occurred around 550 AD, it still poses a threat. An avalanche on November 10, 1993, claimed the lives of ten elite climbers. This travesty is still considered the worst climbing accident in Ecuador.

Loja - *population 404,835*

At 7,300 feet (2225 m), this province is home to many microclimates and environments including cloud forest, jungle, and highlands.

The city of Loja is growing as an expat destination. For now, it remains a quiet and authentic Ecuadorian town with small pockets of gringos. It's known best for its music, often called the musical capital of Ecuador. Many of the country's best musicians matriculated from Loja, plus the city has two orchestras and a music conservatory!

Keep in mind, there is very little English spoken here. As there are no stereotypes or attitudes towards gringos yet, they are more easily accepted into the community. The weather is ideal with days reaching low to mid 70s F (21 C) and nights averaging a low of 45 degrees F (7 C).

In addition to ideal weather, Loja boasts some amazing natural assets! There are green mountain peaks, valleys, rushing rivers and plenty of places to farm potatoes and corn.

As with many small towns, this one is safe! You can feel free to walk around the town even into the night. Even in safe towns, I believe the

saying, *"Nothing good ever happens after midnight."*

Plus, you don't need a car to accomplish everyday tasks. The town is easy to navigate by foot, and taxis are plentiful usually running $1 USD to anywhere in town.

Vilcabamba

Vilcabamba, just south of Loja, is an up-and-coming expat location. It's also a common weekend getaway for Ecuadorians. Some Sundays it's so popular that it's impossible to find a parking spot! The town is nicknamed *"Playground of the Inca"* because it was once used as a retreat for Incan royalty. If it was fit for royalty, it could very well be worth adding to your research and exploration trip itinerary.

Vilcabamba is slowly attracting more expat "hippie" types who are drawn to the rumors that claim inhabitants often live 100 years and longer. This rumor has yielded yet another knick-name, *"Valley of Longevity."* This rumor has been studied by scientists and we now believe that the fruit, roots, and herbs of this particular Equatorial region offer some of the strongest anti-oxidant protection in the world. The drinking water in the region also has a unique balance of colloidal minerals that, apparently, *does a body OLD*. Other scientists believe that the amazing *old age* is a result of the villagers' poor recollection, stating that the average inhabitant claiming the

age of 100 or higher was, in fact, approximately 86.

Pichincha - *population 2,576,799*

This province is home to a UNESCO World Heritage City,

Quito. It's also home to the largest international airport in Ecuador (UIO). Mariscal Sucre International Airport was completed and opened for business in February of 2013.

Quito

Quito is a diverse and cosmopolitan city. It caters to those that like the big city life with countless entertainment options. There are numerous free concerts offered by the National Symphony Orchestra. There are also parks and trails for biking and walking. With the Andes nearby, a day hike is just a few minutes away. Big mountains like Pichincha, Cayambe, and Cotopaxi are also very close by. Andean towns Otavalo and Papallacta

are popular day trip destinations from Quito.

Public transportation in the city is excellent. They have a metro that has a dedicated lane that slices through the traffic thereby taking no time at all, costing only a quarter!

The shopping is phenomenal, and there are numerous international food options. There is also a good supply of affordable apartments for rent. All of your needed amenities, entertainment options, and more are located in this UNESCO World Heritage City!

Imbabura - *population 333,000*

The province is named after the volcano of the same name, Imbabura, since its peaks along with Cotacachi

and Mojanda volcanoes flank the town (4,630m or 15,190ft).

Otavalo

Otavalo is home to arguably the best textile[13] markets in South America. Their Sunday market is famous across the continent and includes 90 concrete umbrella stands. In addition to awesome thread, there is a vibrant cultural energy here. The town is welcoming and authentic. Even with shoppers passing through, they have found a way to stick to their roots which is exactly what made them famous!

Otavalo is primarily a farming and artisan community. With the influx in tourism, new hotels, hostels, and tour operators have popped up around town. Also, we have seen an increase in the production of handicrafts.

Cotacachi

Cotacachi is just a short bus ride away from Otavalo. In

---

[13] handmade blankets, tablecloths, and much more

fact if you are traveling by bus to Cotacachi, you will need to change buses in Otavalo. Entering the town feels like you are stepping back in time. Here you are not concerned with your wifi signal, instead you are mesmerized with the blend of indigenous and the mestizo majority. You will hear just about as much Quechua as Spanish spoken. The indigenous are very friendly people and jump towards opportunities to show others their great way of life.

One example of their traditions include dressing in all white and carrying a white rabbit to the house of the woman you wish to marry with the entire town in tow. If the father of the woman you wish to marry accepts the rabbit, the whole town proceeds together to the ceremony. Everyone wears white and everyone parties!

The town is famous for its leather production and leather shopping. There is a main street filled with top class shops selling leather purses,

jackets, shoes, etc. There is also an outdoor market on the weekends where you will see textile and leather goods.

There is a breathtaking crater lake nearby, **Cuicocha**.[14] The sapphire blue laguna is believed by the indigenous to be bottomless, but Wikipedia says it's 200 m (656 ft). Its name translates to "Rainbow Lake."

The largest festival in Cotacachi, Into Raymi (Sun Festival), begins the day before summer solstice commemorating the history between the indigenous and the mestizo majority. Sometimes this festival gets too rowdy, and long stemmed frustrations lead to rock throwing. The second day of the festival, indigenous shamans use Cuicocha as a bath for ritual cleansing and purification. I'll bet it's especially needed after some old tensions resurface!

Even though I just mentioned stone throwing, the people really are kind and proud of their town. They have a

---

[14] Watch a 1 min video of Laguna Cuicocha here: http://bit.ly/cuicochalake

quiet disposition and are very friendly.

I had some of the best hot chocolate I've ever had here. It gets cold at night. I had a small electric heater in my room, and I still packed on the alpaca blankets!

Tungurahua - *population 504,034*

Tungurahua is filled with volcanos, waterfalls, lively energy, and tourists! To be fair, the tourists are mostly congregated in the **Baños** area. A location known for gorgeous waterfalls, hot springs, and a killer mountain biking stretch that is straight downhill for miles!

If one volcano isn't enough for you, try three! Tungurahua, Carihuayrazo, and Chimborzo volcanos surround you in this canton. The main river, Patate, dissects east towards the Amazon region. There's a unique feel in the air from the power dispersed by the volcanos, fresh flowing water, and strong indigenous influences. The US issued an advisory regarding Tungurahua volcano due to its recent eruption on February 3rd, 2014 and "a period of high activity that includes emissions of ash and pyroclastic flows (fast-moving currents of hot gas and rock)." To monitor the activity of the volcanos and earthquakes in Ecuador the spanish website, Ecuadorian Geophysical Institute, provides the most accurate and up-to-date information complete with live volcano cameras.

The climate in the region is temperate, often wet and cool, yet is also known as the gateway to the hot and humid Amazon. From Baños you can easily jump to Puyo, Misahuallí, Ines Maria, Pailon del Diablo, and the waterfalls of Agoyan.

Outdoor enthusiasts should definitely explore Baños and the surrounding area as a potential landing zone. Trekking, kayaking, white-water rafting, mountain biking, and enjoying a soak in the local hot springs after your venture, can all be accomplished in Baños.

Balance out the adrenalin with some cultural events.

Tungurahua is well-known for its Carnival held during the end of February. A walk through town this time of year can lend you to bullfights and parades.

Some tourists add Salasaca to their itinerary in order to pick up high quality, low cost, woolen and sisal rugs and wall hangings!

The capital of this canton is Ambato, "the city of flowers and fruit," which has developed into the leading town of the Ecuadorian Sierra and the 10th largest city in Ecuador. Monday is a great day to visit Ambato and observe tourists and locals alike fill the streets for the food and clothing venders at the weekly market.

AMAZONIA

◆ Population: 6,042,000
◆ Tropical rainforest- lots of rain
◆ Large oil reserves
◆ UNESCO World Heritage Site Sangay National Park
◆ Indigenous tribes

The Amazon, or Oriente, is compiled from the following provinces: Morona Santiago, Napo, Orellana, Pastaza, Sucumbíos, and Zamora-Chinchipe.

This region consists primarily of national parks and indigenous zones. These zones are protected areas for Amazon indigenous tribes to continue living traditionally. Conversely, the region is also home to the largest reserves of petroleum in Ecuador. Much of Ecuador's upper Amazon has been exploited in the search for crude oil.

Since the Amazon is a far off wonderland, many indigenous populations live the same today as they did a hundred years ago. The Shuar, Huaorani, Siona, Secoya, Cofán, and Quechua populations are still alive and well in this wild province. There are also numerous tribes in the deep jungle which are rarely contacted.

As you can image by the name "rainforest," rain is ever present and in massive force. In particular, the Andean piedmont can receive more than 197 inches (5,000mm) a year!

The region is not known as an expat landing zone. However, if you're looking for a blast from the past, hot and wet world, look no further. Well, a little further. Below are the descriptions of the provinces and major cities.

Morona-Santiago -

population 115,324

This province has very little infrastructure. It's a main entry point for tourists seeking an Amazon experience. However, it remains unexploited due to inefficient transportation options. Its primary economy is based on visitors to Sangay National Park and the indigenous town of Shuara.

Sangay National Park is a UNESCO World Heritage site that features two active volcanos and a tropical rainforest that lays alongside glaciers and snow-capped mountains! The park spans across three provinces (Tungurahua and Chimborazo are the remaining two provinces). One of the few places in the world where you can see jaguars, condors, speckled bear, giant otters, and mountain tapirs.[15]

Macas

Macas, named after the Macas Indians, is the capital of the province and lies in the Upano Valley overlooking the Upano river. The city is important to indigenous communities since political federations that protect them use Maca as a hub. It's also an important region for the production of: yuca, sugarcane, papaya, coffee, and bananas.

Over the last few years, Macas has entered the tourism market offering jungle treks,

---

[15] More on the World Heritage site: http://whc.unesco.org/en/list/260

trips to indigenous communities, and white-water rafting!

Napo - *population 79,139*

This province is primarily comprised of indigenous and isolated communities (its capital excluded). Outside of its capital, Tena, it is undeveloped and thereby an industrial presence. Napo is known for its thick rainforest that is home to numerous tribes. This province hosts the Antisana Ecological Reserve[16]and Limoncocha National Biological Reserve.[17]

Tena

Most of the population in Napo live in Tena, a surprisingly friendly and industrialized town in an otherwise unindustrialized province! There's a major hospital, tourism businesses, a small airport, and a bus terminal. Since there is some infrastructure in place, it has served as a popular launching point for jungle treks, kayaking, and rafting! Tena has a friendly, peaceful and clean reputation. It's certainly considered tourist-ready!

Tena is surrounded with forested hills and the Andes on its west flank. It's no wonder tourists make the journey. Expats can dive into volunteer projects ranging from reforestation to development initiatives. Plus, two major confederations that protect the indigenous communities are based in Tena: Fonakin[18] and Ashin.[19]

You can have a true cultural experience after hours. It isn't uncommon to see volunteers, guides, and indigenous people dancing together to reggae, salsa, and pop music.

---

[16] More on Antisana Ecological reserve: http://www.getquitoecuador.com/quito-natural-attractions/antisana_volcano.html

[17] More on Limoncocha Ecological reserve: http://www.ecuador.com/protected-areas/limoncocha-reserve/

[18] Federación de Organizaciones de la Nacionalidad Kichwa de Napo

[19] Asociación de Shamanes Indígenas de Napo

Orellana - *population 136,000*

This province is primarily jungle with crude oil, timber, and tourism as the primary economic sources. The capital of the province is Puerto Francisco de Orellana, often called Coca (after the nearby Coca River). With a name that long, I can see why!

Puerto Francisco de Orellana

Coca has a small airport and a decent tourist infrastructure with hotels, restaurants, and bars. As you would imagine, most hotels are located riverfront, which is convenient since most transportation is done by boat.

Medical facilities are sparse here. There are only a few walk in clinics: Clinica Sinaí and García Moreno. The latter has the best reputation.

As far as wildlife goes, this place is a mecca. Tourists will see numerous monkey varieties, snakes, great anteaters, jaguars (or more frequently jaguar tracks), and hundreds of other animals.

Pastaza - *population 25,800*

Pastaza is the largest and most biodiverse province in Ecuador!

El Puyo

El Puyo is the capital of this province and also a picture perfect town. Located between Baños and Macas, this town is popular for commercial, cultural, and political centers of the Amazonia region. Razor-sharp mountains descend upon rivers that lazily drain towards the vibrant Amazon. The name, Puyo, is a Quechan word that translates to cloudy. This mountain Amazonian hybrid of a town is wet and overcast with an average of less than ten dry days a month!

As you travel east along the province, you'll leave the mountains behind. In their place is a relatively flat topography, rich with rivers and plains and more rain near the Peruvian border.

Sucumbíos - *population 144,774*

Sucumbíos is the only province in Ecuador that shares borders with two countries, Peru and Colombia. The indigenous culture were the only people who called it home for most of history. That was until oil was discovered.

The largest city and base for oil drilling operations is located in Nueva Loja, more commonly referred to as *Lago Agrio*. A small oil company called Texaco (now owned by Chevron) is based in Lago Agrio.

Lago Agrio

This area is an environmental nightmare. The rainforest is a thing of the past,

and oil pollution is catastrophic. On Valentine's Day, 2011, an Ecuadorian judge ruled that Chevron had to pay $9 billion in environmental damages. Sadly, I doubt the money trickled down to repair the ravaged environment.

The area is not known on the tourist circuit due to the damage to the natural habitat. Sucumbíos is the first Ecuadorian province to suffer massive exploitation.

Zamora-Chinchipe

This province is the southern mountainous jewel of Ecuador's Amazon region. It borders Peru to the east and south. Instead of oil, it's known for the longevity of its residents, gold-mining, indigenous groups alongside expats, tourism, birding, massive rivers, and gorgeous waterfalls!

Zamora

Zamora is the capital of the province and an up-and-coming expat town. Tucked away in the foothills of the magnificent Andes Mountains, there are numerous natural assets that make Zamora a gorgeous place to pass time.

Three large rivers: Zamora, Bombuscaro, and Jamboé converge in the city. Along with them, they bring magnificent waterfalls and a constant influx of exotic birds, lending the city to the knick-name *"City of Birds and Waterfalls."*

Zamora is currently experiencing an economic boom due to the discovery of gold in the surrounding region a few years back. The weather is superior to many of the other Amazonian options, possibly due to the altitude and mountainous topography. The highs average between 73 - 79 F (23 - 26 C) and lows

from 57 - 60 F (14 - 16 C) year-round. The rain is a different story as well, only averaging 10 days of rain or less per month.

The locals are friendly and haven't been turned off by a massive influx of transplants... yet.

Ecuadorians, in general, do not appreciate the "hippie" look. They take great care with their hygiene and appearance and often are turned off by those who do not. If you are looking for the most hospitable experience, lose the dreads.

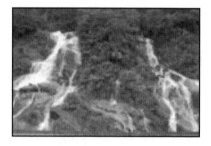

TRY BEFORE YOU PRY

How renting prior to buying in your desired location can save you bucket loads, and renting vs. buying your dream home

I was a 911 paramedic in my "last life." In the emergency medical field, the mantra "Try before you pry" was a common and important one. When we approached a residence or car at an accident, we always attempted to gain entry by turning the handle before we broke the door down. This practice resulted in less damage and an overall better experience. The same can be true for your experience launching as an expat, you should peak past the door before you commit. Spending a year trying on a country could save you tons of money and psychological damage.

Try it on

Ecuador may intoxicate you with numerous natural assets, prices that cause your mouth to drop, and a pace that resonates with something inside of you. Which is why, after a brief visit, many people find themselves snatching up property while wearing "tourist goggles." Buying a house or property in Ecuador should *NEVER* be done on a whim.

First off, you might be tricked if you don't do your homework. Second, you are viewing EC as a tourist. You really should live in your desired region for at least six months, better yet a year, to learn if it's a good fit. While renting a property, evaluate the area as a local and see what it's like after the honeymoon phase is over. Things like how often the water and electricity go out can re-direct your opinion on life in any particular region. Then, and only then, can you make a fully informed decision.

TIP

"The most important advice from the owner of EcuaAssist to soon-to-be expats was, "First rent and spend a year here, then if you are comfortable, make the decision to move."
~ Dr. Marcos Chiluisa
EcuaAssist.com

More often than not, those that leave Ecuador with discouragement and contempt for the country are those who didn't do their homework, foot on the ground. Their expectations did not reflect the life that Ecuador provides. It's a common problem, because most literature out there is tied to sales. You read about Ecuador through a real estate agent's eyes, or through someone who sells familiarisation tours. Take a deep breath, and read these words exactly as they come. The only thing I sold you is a book that I hope will guide you towards or away from Ecuador, depending on how you respond to the unfiltered truth.

Certainly, there are times when you perform all your due diligence and Ecuador is just not the right fit for you. Many more times, however, people make the romantic leap into a tropical paradise without researching what exactly it entails. I can guarantee you, *it won't be a tropical version of your hometown!*

Research online as much as you'd like, but I dare to declare that it doesn't amount to enough. Not until you forge through the country and experience an Ecuadorian life will you truly understand the consequences both good and bad of your decision. For some, life in Ecuador looked better on *House Hunters International* than it played out in real life.

I enthusiastically urge you to budget an exploratory trip to experience different regions, and try them out by renting a place in each contending town. That way, when you do decide which region is your slice of heaven, you can rest easy knowing you have explored the country and your city is not only great, but better than all of the other good options you explored.

If you think that trekking around the country is not worth the cost or time, think again. Consider the added stress and cost of selling the house you regretfully purchased. Think of the life in your home country you sold away only to crawl back to

later. You might be stuck in a foreign world for years before you can sell.

If you have an opportunity to rent the property you are thinking of purchasing, then all the better! You can see if the house is well built, if the plumbing and electricity are problematic, and ascertain the cost of general upkeep. Meanwhile if another buyer enters the scene, you would be given the opportunity to offer a bid of your own if you felt so inclined. A true win-win!

RENT

There is no denying my bias towards renting. The benefits are numerous!

- Try out the area with little to no commitment.
- Little financial investment, usually only requiring a deposit and first month's rent.
- Peace of mind that if something breaks, and it always does, you are not the one footing the bill.

- If you don't like your residence, community, or family circumstances no longer permit you to stay, you are free to pick up and leave.
- If the property proves to be a lemon, you can leave.
- If you are sensitive to the energy of a place, you can try it on and decide if you thrive there.

If you opt to rent make sure and ask the following questions:

- What your rental rate includes (homeowner fee, water, electric, tv cable, gas)
- Ask for an inventory list. Don't assume that just because your condo doesn't have a coffee maker you will get one. You accept the unit as is. If you don't like something about the unit, negotiate changes before you sign.

Other common myths:
- If you decide to spend money on your own accord to "improve" the condo, don't

assume you will be reimbursed.
- If you break your rental lease for whatever reason (even a death in the family), *you lose your security deposit*.

BUY

Just because I am clearly pro-renting before buying does not mean buying is without benefit:

- Continuity
- You are free to create your customized oasis, the dream home you alway wanted
- Potential path for immigration (see the *Immigration* section)
- You have potential rental income
- You don't throw away money on rent (something that doesn't contribute towards ownership)
- You can personalize the heck out of your house
- A chance to gain equity if the value rises, which if you're in it for the long haul, is very likely to happen

• Often, a lower monthly housing expense, that is fixed and could be paid off over time

Take home message here? *Try before you pry* and your cost of living will not include a $150K debt!!

EXPAT EXPERIENCE

There was a couple who wanted to spend $150k or less on a penthouse apartment in Cuenca. This price point was not realistic for what they wanted. However, they found a deal that was "too good to be true." (*In Ecuador, when a deal is too good to be true, walk away*) Well, it was too good to be true. After they moved all of their belongings into the penthouse, the water tanks the apartment was built on ruptured and their apartment along with their belongings were destroyed.

COST OF LIVING

THIS SECTION HAS BEEN STRESS TESTED BY EXPATS ON THE GROUND!

Cost of living all depends on what the "good life" looks like to you. No matter what lifestyle you choose, the corresponding cost will be less in Ecuador than North America. Sure there are things that are more expensive, like electronics, but overall you will save cash. Your savings jump if you opt to live where A/C or heat is not necessary.

See the following budget for a family of two living in a two bedroom, one bath apartment in Cuenca to provide a starting point for your financial expectations. Since the couple are in a pedestrian friendly town, they opted not to purchase a car. This budget demonstrates one way to live.

MONTHLY EXPENSES

Rent: $450
Water bill: $8
Electric Bill: $50
Cell Phone: $20
Transportation: $20
Groceries: $200

Drinks out: $30
Cable Internet/TV: $50
Supplemental Healthcare: $80

Monthly total= $908

EXPAT EXPERIENCE

"Many expats arrive in Ecuador believing they can live on $400-$500 dollars a month here because of something they read in International Living. That's just not true."
~ Dr. Chiluisa
EcuaAssist

HOUSING

Oftentimes the hardest part about finding your dream home is deciding what in the world that looks like! Make a list of your must haves and your highly desired qualities in a home. Really think on this. I've heard many realtors express that a high percentage of their clients have no clue what they want. Do you want little-to-no upkeep, to live in a gated or resort community, or are you looking for a farm with fruit trees and a garden to get dirty in? Do you envision living amongst other expats or fully integrating with the locals?

Keep in mind that some communities are more geared toward the part-time expat, meaning features and security may vary according to the season. It is very likely your neighbors inside gated communities will fluctuate, since many expats "snow-bird" and others decide it's not for them and return to their "motherland."

Depending on your personality, and if your Spanish is not so bueno, you will either opt to immerse yourself in the Ecuadorian community to learn the language or hideaway in the "gringo-ville" of your choosing.

RENT

There are many considerations when searching for an apartment/house for rent. Secondary to location, my biggest concern is "Is it furnished?" Unfurnished in Ecuador means bare bones. No appliances, often not even a stove! However, fully furnished can include everything: linens, cookware, furniture, etc. Just bring your toothbrush, gadgets, and clothes. If you opt to rent an unfurnished place, it isn't extraordinarily expensive to furnish in Ecuador.

Brian, from Florida, bought a stove, fridge, microwave oven, dining table, four kitchen chairs, queen pillow top mattress and frame for just under $2,000! That price was paid using a bilingual local who chose the shop which means he scored a decent commission!

TIP

Many expat hubs in Ecuador are at high altitudes, which means you will be cooking at altitude, so make corresponding adjustments to your recipes. Owning a pressure cooker could really be an asset in Cuenca.

There is an outstanding market for rental homes in EC. You can rent anything from a million dollar mansion that overlooks the Pacific to a humble local-styled cabina in the mountains. Whether you choose to pay $350 to $3,000 per month is up to your lifestyle! Most expats I have interviewed

pay between $400-$750 a month in rent.

While shopping around, make sure to inquire if there are A/C units in each room, central air, or fans only. Central air is nice, but much more expensive since you are cooling the entire house instead of just the room you are in. Before you sign a lease, and while you still have negotiating power, see if you can get the utilities included in your rent. This makes for a simplistic rental experience when you don't have to open new accounts with cable providers or hunt down the water company to pay your $8.00 bill.

EXPAT EXPERIENCE

"We traded a small one bedroom condo in Houston for a large three bedroom, four bath home on the beach. I'd say we did good."
~ Connie Wilson, expat from Houston

Below are a few examples of rentals on the market when this book was written:

✳ "Nice 2bd/1ba apartment in the most exclusive area of the city center of **Cuenca**, next to YANUNCAY river in the touristic-cultural sector. Close to: museums, exhibitions, restaurants, bars, theaters, bank, parks, shop and others. Fully furnished, two comfortable bedrooms with closets, bathroom, dining room, spacious kitchen, and beautiful garden. $550 USD, includes hot and cold water, electricity, telephone, cable TV, internet, gas, and rent."

✳ "Beautiful and comfortable fully furnished 1bd/1ba apartment with terrace near Bicentennial Park (**Quito**). It is located in the north of the city. Near the apartment there are supermarkets and pharmacies to buy, as well as many shops and bakeries. You can easily walk to anything that you need. $340 includes internet, linens, and cooking utensils."

✳ "This is the ultimate condo. In upscale San Lorenzo, (Salinas) on the northern and quiet end of the Malecon/ esplanade/beach. It's within a few minutes walk to all restaurants, stores and clubs. This 3 bedroom turn-key 2100 sq ft. (195 meters) condo, which occupies the entire 5th floor of the building is only $1500 a month! It is large, has high ceilings, is meticulously and beautifully furnished and decorated.

It has 35 feet of wall to wall, floor to ceiling windows and sliders to capture the spectacular panoramic views of Salinas Bay, the beach, and the Yacht club. Each of the three bedrooms are spacious master suites, each with its own ensuite bathroom and custom walk-in closet. There is also a separate powder room. The large and light eat in kitchen has the latest upscale stainless steel appliances and plenty of counter room for preparation.

The view from the kitchen window is out to the Salinas Yacht Club on the Bay. The condo comes completely equipped with everything you need including a laundry room with a full size washer and dryer, cable TV and high speed internet. This condo building comes with a parking space, doorman, and 24/7 security and staff."

CLOSING COSTS

Closing costs are usually the responsibility of the buyer but can be negotiated to be shared between the buyer and seller. Costs may vary depending on the complexity of the transaction and location or canton. Make sure to ask your specialist, or attorney, to itemize the anticipated closing costs.

Once you select the perfect property, be prepared to dole out part or all of the following closing costs (the figures below are estimates and could vary greatly from a large city to a small town):

+ Purchase Agreement (Lawyer Fee) $250 +
+ Purchase Agreement (Notary Fee) $50 - $100
+ Minuta (Lawyer Fee) $150
+ Alcabala (Tax 1%) $500
+ Property Deed (Notary Fee) $150 - $250
+ Property Registration (Government Fee) $350 - $560

Total Estimated Closing Costs = $1,450

If you use a buyer's agent, tack on the industry standard fee of 3%.

PROPERTY TAXES

Your annual property taxes, or *Predio*, vary depending on your location but average 0.1% of the property's *assessed value*. Clearly, much lower than the States! Since the assessed value is often a fraction of what you paid, you save from every direction!

UTILITIES

Water is easily accessed and very affordable. An average water bill will run $8-15 a month. Electric varies greatly, however, if you are running an A/C unit or two non-stop, you may look forward to a bill as high as $200. If you aren't home much, eat out, and don't run a dryer, your only anticipated cost is $20-30 a month. Internet averages between $35-45 and is often DSL. Gasoline is also inexpensive, only *$1.48 per gallon*, about $4 less than in Costa Rica! The average fuel expense for a family of three is about $40-60 per month.

FOOD

Food costs can be extremely affordable if you utilize Ecuador's famed fresh produce for the bulk of your grocery needs. If instead, you prefer comfort foods imported from North America, you will need to budget for it! Many items, like Cheetos, are more than 3x the cost in Ecuador. If you eat like a local (rice, beans, soup, fresh produce, small portions of meat), your monthly food expense can run less than $170 p/mo (for a family of two). If you eat out a lot or need some comfort food from home, expect to pay up to double.

TRANSPORTATION

BUS

The bus system is extensive in Ecuador. There is a bus to get you just about anywhere. Travel usually runs between 1 - 1.5x longer than by car. So, if it usually takes one hour to travel from Salinas to Guayaquil by car, then expect it to take close to two hours by bus.

They are cheap, relatively clean and economic, running about $1 per hour of driving. Make sure to bring change since it's often difficult for the driver to break large bills.

Vendors will often pop on board and sell you mangos, fresh juices, popsicles, water, agua de pipa (coconut water), and more for mere pennies. Most beverages are served in plastic baggies. It may seem weird at first, but once you learn the system of biting a hole in the bottom corner, it makes a lot of sense.

TAXI

Taxis are plentiful in the larger cities and near tourist attractions. Keep in mind if you are in Guayaquil or Quito to use precautions. See the *Crime* section for more information.

If you have ventured off the beaten path, it's usually still possible to hire a cab by asking the restaurant or hotel to call one. It's always best to stick with marked taxis. Make sure to negotiate the rate before you enter the cab. A two-hour ride will run you anywhere from $90-110 depending on your negotiating skills in Spanish and how busy the day has been for your driver. Short runs around town will cost you a buck.

RENTAL CARS

In order to rent a car, you must be: 25 or older, have a valid driver's license, passport, and credit card with at least $1000 - $2000 spending room. That's all pretty standard stuff,

so let me share with you the potential surprises.

There is no CDW (Collision Damage Waiver), instead they tack on a 12% tax and insurance fee once you are at their counter with the credit card in your hot little hands. If your rental pick up is at an airport, you can expect to pay an additional 8% fee. So, to sum it up, you can expect up to 20% in additional fees on top of what your reservation quotes you.

VEHICLE COSTS

- Initial Purchase
- Fuel **$1.48 p/gallon**
- Car Registration
- SOAT Insurance
- Inspection
- Repairs

CAR MATRICULATION (Registration)[20]

Each car cruising the streets of Ecuador needs to maintain its matriculation by paying an annual fee (*except*

---

[20] http://bit.ly/registrationEC

tourists who are traveling through the country on a tourist visa). The fee includes: a property and environmental tax (both administered by the SRI) and a registration fee (Transit Commission of Ecuador).

A quick visit to their site[21] will show you the range of fees is from $0 - $70 and varies directly with the value of the car. The range of car values starts at $1000 USD and caps at $40,001 USD.

If you purchase your car new, the marketer must send the sale information to SRI. Once the information is validated, you will need to venture to a financial institution that has a working relationship with the SRI and pay your registration.

When you purchase a used car, and every year after your first year of a new car purchase, you will need to renew your matriculation on the month which is based on the last digit of your license plate, or *placa*. See the following table.

Month	Last Digit of Plate
Feb	ending in 1
Mar	ending in 2
April	ending in 3
May	ending in 4
June	ending in 5
July	ending in 6
Aug	ending in 7
Sept	ending in 8
Oct	ending in 9
Nov	ending in 0

SOAT- Mandatory Car Insurance[22]

SOAT stands for *Seguro Obligatorio de Accidentes de Tránsito*. This is an emergency insurance that covers medical expenses resulting from car accidents. According to their website, the insurance covers up to $2,500 USD per victim and event, $50 USD per person per event transported by ambulance, up to $3,000 USD

---

[21] http://bit.ly/registrationEC

[22] For more information see their website: www.soatecuador.info

for permanent *total* disability per person per event, and up to $5,000 USD per death victim. SOAT will also reimburse funeral expenses up to $400 USD per victim.

Like I said before, it's mandatory but don't sweat it, the fees are modest, averaging $10 per month. According to their site, the cost can range from $29.78 - $165.97 a *year*! Calculate your cost by visiting their site and clicking on Cuanto Cuesta. *Spanish skills are required.*

To purchase your SOAT, all you need is the vehicle registration for the car and cold hard cash. No vehicle inspection is required. Simply visit a SOAT office, authorized insurance office, or kiosk at your local mall to buy your SOAT.

This insurance covers anyone who drives your car. It's associated with the car, not the operator. So if you're a generous guy/gal and want to share your wheels, your pals are covered.

What's not covered is damage to your vehicle or material property damage, so think long and hard before you hand over your keys.

EXPAT EXAMPLE

Bryan Haines shared on Gringos Abroad that he pays about $63 USD a year for his SOAT and $80 a month in fuel expense for a 1994 Isuzu Trooper with a 3.2L V6 engine, driving approximately 1200km / 746 miles a month.

REPAIRS

Repairs are inevitable. Between thick clay, bumpy roads, MacGyver fixes and humidity, something is bound to fail. Electrical systems are incessantly difficult to manage. That's why it's good to purchase a car with as few electrical components as possible. If your car is newer or more specialized, it will cost more to repair. My mechanical problems are more often electrical in nature, but I've had my fair share of other problems such as: brake issues, my drive shaft fell out, and even a wheel dislodged and rolled away while driving (1980 CJ7 Jeep)!

DOMESTIC HELP

This is a common splurge in which expats indulge. The cost will vary depending on region and from person to person. The average cost is between $10-25 for 4-5 hours of cleaning which includes sweeping, mopping, cleaning the bathrooms and windows, taking out the trash, etc!

EXPAT EXPERIENCE

"I have a maid come in every two weeks. We paid her $10 for 5 hours, plus an extra $1 for the bus trip that costs a quarter. She scrubs from top to bottom in a 2500 sq ft, 4 bedroom home. Each time she asks me if I wanted her to cook, or do laundry.

Another girl I use since we have moved from Salinas to Puerto Cayo is $20 a day. She cooks, cleans, and does the windows. We are on the beach, and everything needs to be scrubbed constantly. I always feed her lunch and give her a beer."
~ Diane Bublack, expat from West Virgina

MEDICAL CARE

Ecuador is a "Medical Tourism" destination, noted for its low cost, high quality health care.

Even as a tourist, I was able to capitalize on their medical care. My wife had increased pain from cysts in her hands. They x-rayed her hands and prescribed her an anti-inflammatory for free! We were shocked, then we took the prescription for the anti-inflammatory to the pharmacy and were handed said pills for free! We couldn't believe it!

If you don't want to wait through "the system" to see a specialist or undergo a deemed optional procedure, then you can purchase a voluntary plan for just $70 USD per month. The government changed the program in early 2014 by removing the age limit and excluding pre-existing illnesses, making the program open to all! Read more about the healthcare options in the *Healthcare* section.

MEDICATION

Ecuador doesn't have the pharmaceutical giants that own their democratic process (like in the US) so prices remain reasonable. Ok, I'll admit that was a very loaded statement, but can you blame me? There are some medications that are only made in North America and Europe, thereby resulting in a higher cost. Most of your medications are included in your plan in Ecuador.

PART III

LOGISTICS

FROM THEORETICAL TO UNPACKING YOUR SUITCASE

BEFORE YOU ARRIVE

Moving is always listed in the top factors that cause stress. Think back to the last time you moved. Take a few deep breaths, I'm sorry to bring back such a horrific memory. In order to minimize the stress, cost, and errors, organization is essential. While I don't mean to belittle large domestic moves, you will have new obstacles like customs, passports, visas, immigration paperwork, and language barriers!

Not to worry, hundreds of people have successfully moved to Ecuador before you. We gathered all of their tips, and learned from their mistakes to bring you the following pages. Keep an eye out for checklists throughout this section.

SQUARE UP DEBTS

Living abroad is infinitely more possible and manageable without debt. The heaviest anvils weighing you down are your credit card, car payment, mortgage, and school loan debts (if applicable).

Create a new budget and ditch as many "wants" as you can, leaving only your needs. If you have decided to embark on an international life in Ecuador then relocating to Ecuador is now your biggest *want,* so keep that in mind when you sacrifice small things like HBO or cable.

In addition to ditching cable, start brown-bagging again and watch the savings pile up. Look at what you're eating. Almost every Ecuadorian meal includes rice, beans, and soup. If you start eating like an Ecuadorian, you will tighten the belt on your budget and your pants!

When you sell your car, consider using some of the money to pay off credit card debt. Ecuador has decent public transit and many towns are pedestrian friendly. You can save up for another car after you arrive or buy a scooter.

How to Retire Happy [23]by Stan Hinden delves deeper into ways to convert debt into retirement savings.

SECURE DOCUMENTS

After reading the *Immigration* section, if you qualify for a cedula, make sure to secure all the paperwork needed before your departure. This will save months of frustration and hundreds of dollars.[24]

If your driver's license or passport are going to expire soon, renew them now so they arrive before you depart! If you have children, make sure their passports and visa documentation

---

[23] http://bit.ly/retirehappy

[24] see Immigration for more information on required paperwork

are in order before your departure.

Also you will read in the **Ecuadorian Driver's License** section that you need an apostilled letter from the transit authority in your home country in order to obtain a driver's license, so make sure and grab that before you leave.

FOUR-LEGGED FRIENDS

Bringing pets into Ecuador is a fairly easy process as long as your pet isn't a part or full Pit Bull or Rottweiler breed. Ecuador absolutely does not allow either of these breeds or their mixes through their front door!

As long as you have the proper documentation (see below), your pets will not be quarantined. Ecuador only allows admittance of two pets per person.

If you show up without proper paperwork, it could end badly. One of the following scenarios would play out. Your pet would be quarantined, refused entry, or sent back to

the country of origin, all at the owner's expense.

I discovered numerous discrepancies regarding the exact process for achieving the correct paperwork during my research. I wrote to the Embassy in Washington D.C. and asked them to spell out the procedure. This is what they had to say:

"First, visit your local veterinarian; make sure that the office has the International U.S Department of Agriculture form #7001. This is very important: If the vet does not have the proper form, he must contact the USDA office to have them send the form. This is a government document that can only be requested by a certified veterinarian. For the physical exam of the pet, bring any medical documents, especially records of vaccines.

Second, if time permits, mail the completed form to the USDA office. If not enough time, then call the office for an appointment. Visit the office and bring all of your documents including the vaccine record, form #7001, and also the vet certificate of good health. This office will notarize and give permission to export your pet from the USA.

Third, you must visit the Consulate of Ecuador to have the above Form #7001 legalized. Legalization fee: $50.00, no personal checks will be accepted.

Finally, remember that the form 7001 will be valid only for 10 days from the issuance date.

To Sum Up Four-Legged Logistics:

☐ Get a Health Certificate (USDA form 7001) from your vet, **issued within 10 days of travel** by a USDA or CFIA accredited vet (North Americans). If your vet is not the area's head honcho, then send the form to the area vet with a note indicating that the pet is going to Ecuador. Once the form is approved, either mail or walk the form into the nearest Ecuadorian Consulate / Embassy with a $50 money order. You will receive a fancy stamped document that provides permission to bring your pets. The Embassy reports that this document is only good for 10 days after it is awarded, but many expats are reporting that it acts like a pet visa that lasts for 21 days. When in doubt, I always recommend leaning on the conservative number so that you are better prepared.

☐ Dogs: proof of vaccination against distemper (Carre), hepatitis, parovirus (DHLPP), leptospirosis, parainfluenza, parvovirus, and rabies

☐ Cats: feline viral rhinotrachetis, panleukopenia (FVRCP), calicivirus, and rabies

☐ All vaccines except rabies must be administered *within 30 days* of departure to EC

☐ Rabies vaccines must be given *more than 30 days* but less than *12 months* prior to traveling to EC. The three-year rabies vaccine is not recognized in EC

☐ Tick & Tapeworm test must be completed within 21 days prior to travel

After arriving in Ecuador, your pet must undergo an examination at the port of entry. If your pet is found to be free of any evidence of disease communicable to humans, you will be good to go! If the vet finds something suspect, further examination by a licensed vet may be required, and it will be funded with your dime.

Other Animals:

Birds, invertebrates, tropical fish, reptiles, amphibia, rodents, and rabbits do not need to show rabies vaccination but may have other requirements in addition to the Health Certificate in order to enter Ecuador.

If you have an exotic animal or one not listed here, make sure and visit, call, or email your closest Ecuadorian Embassy.[25]

Pet Logistics

Microchipping dogs and cats has become a regular practice. It makes sense to have this done if you haven't already. A microchip is a surefire way to prove ownership and is required for some pet transporter companies. However, it's not required to gain entry into Ecuador.

Once you have gathered your paperwork and have chipped your pets, you are ready to shop for the best transportation for them. Make sure you are well versed in your airline's pet transport policy before you purchase your tickets! Some airlines restrict weight limits for in-cabin pets. Other restrictions often include maximum and minimum outdoor temperatures, nonstop flight requirement, and / or breed restrictions.

A good starting point would be to review the pet policies of the airlines that service Ecuador from North America below.

PET POLICIES

United:
http://bit.ly/unitedpetpolicy

American:
http://bit.ly/americanpetpolicy

Delta:
http://bit.ly/deltapetpolicy

US Airways:
http://bit.ly/ USairwayspetpolicy

LAN:
http://bit.ly/LANpetpolicy

---

[25] http://www.embassypages.com/ecuador

TACA:
http://bit.ly/tacapetpolicy

There are a few different ways to get your loved four-legger to EC. With many airlines, you can carry your smaller pets on board in a pet carrier for a fee. If your pet is a service dog the fee is waved, and the pet does not need a carrier. Make sure you read the airline's policy (the included links) and not a third party's site. During the research for this book, there were numerous out-of-date sources of information. The last thing any pet owner wants is to show up for your flight and learn you can't bring your four-legged baby.

If you have a service dog or therapy dog, they can board with you with the proper identification without a fee. If your pet is not a service dog, nor do they fit under the seat in a carrier, then your options are restricted to shipping them as checked luggage or hiring a pet transporter.

Pet transportation companies utilize smaller planes that are often temperature regulated. Some even include a vet tech or other caretaker to monitor your furry children, assuring their comfort.

Services like Pet Movers are pricey but will actually deliver your pet door to door! They also provide you with a moving counselor who will help facilitate the best schedule and route so your pet has the fewest connections possible. They provide the kennels used during transit, the kenneling when necessary for customs, shots and paperwork as needed, and obtain international import permits! They are also a member of the IPATA and USDA pet handlers.http://bit.ly/petmovers

Shop around and find the best pet transporter that fits your budget and requirements. There are many scammers in the transportation sector. I recommend visiting www.ipata.org to shop for your transporter. Only reputable pet transporters are awarded certification through the International Pet and Animal

Transportation Association (IPATA). The website also includes information on airlines, insurance, vets, animal handlers and more!

MAIL SYSTEM

You need to reshape your mail to suit your international living.

☐ Make sure you unsubscribe from magazines, catalogs, and other snail mail subscriptions.

☐ Start a list now of people and companies that you will need to advise of your move.

You may believe there are only 10 or 15 people, but I bet that as time progresses, you will think of more and more businesses, friends, and services that need to know about your move.

☐ Set up online billing and electronic statements for your bank, credit cards, student loans, etc.

☐ Sign up for an absentee ballot if you are interested in keeping up with your rights as a US citizen.

☐ If you have a family member or friend that is extremely supportive and wants to lend a hand, ask them to use their address as your US address and have them email you pictures of your mail as it arrives. This favor will require occasional shipping of mail and packages to you. I would recommend sending their favorite sweets via Amazon as a thank you!

☐ Or invest in a mail service that will provide you with a US address, scan pictures of your mail, and allow you to respond with options to trash or ship to you. Expats are reporting Club Correos[26] is a very reliable option for receiving packages from the States including those purchased from online retailers like Amazon. Annual membership is just $11.20. This membership secures you a Miami address where you can ship packages weighing up to 4 kilos and worth $400 in declared value tariff free! ServiEntrega is also a company that ships to Ecuador that has been found to be fairly reliable.

Ecuador is currently revamping import regulations in an attempt to force additional domestic spending and use of the government's correos system. Once in place, the new regulation will charge a $42 fee on each packages less than four kilos and valued at less than $400 that is shipped using any agency other than the correos del Ecuador.

BANKING

Your local credit union or large chain bank might have been an excellent choice for you in your hometown, but as an international bank it may fall short. Re-evaluate your bank with the following criteria designed to suit your new international life.

- Can you fax a wire request to transfer money?
- Are there ATM fees and if so, are they excessive?
- What is the currency transaction fee?
- If you are receiving a pension, Social Security, or annuity, can the payments be automatically deposited to your current bank? (www.ssa.gov/foreign/index.html)
- Do they offer mobile deposits? (the ability to take a picture of both sides of the check and deposit the check without ever sending it in)
- Are they FDIC insured?

---

[26] http://www.correosdelecuador.gob.ec/?p=2497

• Is there a minimum balance requirement to avoid maintenance fees?

Most banks charge a foreign transaction fee (a percentage of your purchase) each time you swipe your debit or credit card in a currency other than that of your country of origin. For example, if your bank charges a 10% currency transaction fee (CTF) and you buy dinner for $35 USD, your currency transaction fee will be $3.50 USD! CTFs add up quickly, as do ATM fees. While Ecuador uses the same currency, it's something to keep in mind in case you plan on traveling to nearby countries.

I didn't think to change banks before I moved abroad. In just six months, I racked up $210.67 USD in fees just to access my money! I now proudly bank with Charles Schwab and pay zero fees *(information to follow)*.

Many places in Ecuador are cash driven. Some small towns don't even have a bank or ATM *(cajero)*. That is the exception

however, most cities have at least one bank.

Check to see what your bank charges each time you access your money from an "out of network" ATM. More often than not, the bank whose ATM you are using will also apply a fee. You could be looking at anywhere between $5-10 USD just to use the ATM!

You might conclude that your bank will not serve you well as an international resource. I have banked with Bank of America, Washington Mutual, and most recently Wells Fargo. I was paying way too much to access my money internationally, so I did some research and found a bank that offers everything I was looking for: Charles Schwab's High Yield Investor's Checking Account. *(I do not receive any kickbacks from CS but would love if you mentioned who sent you to them.)*

Take a look at the benefits:
☑ Zero maintenance fees
☑ Zero minimum balance requirement

☑ ZERO CURRENCY TRANSACTION FEES

☑ Free brokerage account

☑ Mobile deposits

☑ Online banking

☑ UNLIMITED ATM FEE REIMBURSEMENTS- not only do they not charge ATM fees of their own, they take it one step further and reimburse you for the ATM fees other banks charge you to access your money around the world!

The only other time I have heard of ATM fee reimbursement is through small credit unions.

CREDIT CARDS

It is a good idea to have one or two credit cards for emergencies. If you already have your favorite credit cards, make sure they do not expire anytime soon.

Every time I travel at least one of my cards gets turned off due to a fraud alert. Even when I call ahead of time and report my travel plans. Having your cards turned off can be detrimental, which is why I always have three cards. I maintain two credit cards and one debit card, but I never keep all three on my person. I prefer to keep one credit card at home just in case I were to lose it or have my wallet taken from me.

As with your bank, you need to assess your current cards. Do they serve you? I prefer to use credit cards that provide travel rewards and little or no currency transaction fees. Since I travel internationally, I look for cards with rewards for airlines that go to the countries I plan to visit, i.e. American Airlines (One World Alliance) and United (Star Alliance).

I currently use the *Chase Sapphire Preferred* card and the *Mileage Plus Explorer*. Both of these cards dump into the same frequent flier pool. The Sapphire card allows me to transfer my points 1:1 mile into United's Frequent Flier program. You must have decent credit to score the *Chase Sapphire Preferred card*. Another option is the AAdvantage card offered through Citi Bank in conjunction with American

Airlines. I have never enjoyed working with Citi, but I will say it is very easy to redeem your miles anytime on flights around the world. I have flown no fewer than seven times with this card. The longest flight was from Santiago, Chile to Kansas City, USA. I paid $80 in taxes and fuel surcharge and used 30,000 miles! If you have to make a purchase, you might as well make it work for you. The reason I switched to United from American was because American required that either my origin or destination be in the United States. United does not have this requirement.

TIP
Pay attention to additional ways to earn miles. For example, AAdvantage has a dining club you can easily join for free. Once you are a member, you can search for restaurants in your area that participate in the dining club. Each time you dine at a participating restaurant, you accumulate between 3-5 times the miles per dollar spent! It doesn't take long for the points to rack up! Also, they will send an email when they are running additional promotions. I received over 1,000 miles just for clicking the button in my email to sign up for a promotion that allowed me to gain 750 miles by dining twice over the summer!

ALL OF YOUR CRAP

Our belongings can cause a great deal of stress if not dealt with correctly. The first three questions you must ask yourself are: What do I need to take with me? What, if any, select items do I want to ship? Would it make more sense to buy new furnishings or send my house-full in a container? Take a mental inventory of everything in your house. Out of everything in your cupboards, closets, and drawers, how much of it do you actually use on a regular basis? Many people are "collectors" with big houses to fill. Just because you own it does not mean you need to ship it. The hardest decision about moving your belongings is whether to sell or donate everything and start anew, or rent a container and deal with the daunting task of satisfying Ecuador's OCD packing list requirements.

TIP

A common myth is that you cannot ship new appliances such as washer, dryer, and so on in their original packaging. This is simply false. Many expats decide to build a custom home. They ship everything including the kitchen sink, and because they establish it is solely for their use, it is permitted.

STARTING FRESH

A new life with new stuff. You won't have to wait for your belongings to arrive, or deal with the hassles of importing into Ecuador. Instead, you have an open-ended ticket to shop for cool new Ecuadorian furniture. A license to shop!

In essence, you will have undergone a major spring cleaning of your belongings. Your house decor will consist of authentic Ecuadorian furnishings, and selling off

your old stuff could provide a nice chunk of change to help with moving expenses. Most of the time it is cheaper to sell and replace than to ship, especially with the affordability in Ecuador.

If starting fresh is your route, allow a few weeks or months to sell or donate everything outside of what you pack in your suitcases. Conquer one room at a time, leaving the kitchen for last since you will be using kitchen items up until the move.

I'm a 6'0" tall woman which is unheard of in EC. Besides curious stares, it translates to difficulty finding clothes and shoes that fit. Keep that in mind while packing. Ecuadorian men usually range between 5'2-5'6" and women between 4'08"-5'4." Craigslist, eBay, and Facebook are great resources when slimming down your belongings.

While Ecuador has plenty of low cost furniture options, they do not have low cost electronic options! In fact, the newest electronic devices are often double in price or simply not available.

Every situation is different. If you're someone like me, it doesn't make sense to ship a container. I've never been attached to "stuff," outside of my electronics! I have moved regularly every 6 months - 2 years for the last 15 years, so I hadn't accumulated much. The only kitchen item that I move with me is an all purpose cooking knife, or chef's knife (I love to cook) and a magic bullet blender. My furnished condo had everything else that I needed. Your situation may be drastically different, including kids, a house full of furniture, antiques, books that you want to reference, and other items you value and wish to keep.

CONTAINER

If you have the perfect furniture set (bedroom / living room), you don't have to part with it. Nor would you need to figure out where to buy furnishings in a new country with a language barrier. Often Ecuadorian furnishings are not as soft and cozy as furnishings from North America.

If you do choose to move forward with a container, make sure to purchase insurance for the contents. Also, research your moving company. Ask expats for referrals.

Take time to make this decision, it's a big one. If you decide on using a container, make sure you are prepared to wait weeks and sometimes months for your belongings. The average timeframe is 4-8 weeks.

INTERNATIONAL MOVERS

Finding the right moving company is key for any major move. For a move to Ecuador, your moving company can mean the difference from having all of your belongings seized to a seamless tax-free experience. I speak aggressively not to scare you but to share with you the level of seriousness Ecuadorians have regarding imports.

You need to make certain your movers understand the

Ecuadorian import procedures and can walk you through a successful experience based on their track record, specifically in Ecuador.

To begin your research, you can use search aggregators like www.intlmovers.com and www.moverreviews.com. The first allows you to enter your origin and destination locations, and they find companies that service your new and old areas. This allows you to request numerous quotes at once. The second website collects hundreds of reviews for the most popular movers. Compare your quotes to the reviews, BBB,[27] and www.movingscam.com before making a decision.

Ask for references from customers that have shipped to Ecuador from each company you're considering and call them. Question the references about any damage and how the company managed those issues. Ask, *"Were the shippers on time and could you track your shipment throughout the process?"*

These websites are great for generalized moves. Since importing to Ecuador requires specialty knowledge, make sure to do the research to assure your company is well versed and experienced in these rules and regs.

EXPAT EXPERIENCE

"We brought over a container and I wish I would have known that we needed our visas in order to avoid the port taxes. We were supposed to receive a reimbursement since we got our visas within six months of our arrival but we only got $999 of the $1500 back after many months. No one told us that we needed our visas."

~ Joel and Joanna, expats from Illinois

IFE- International Freight Experts[28]

I've read numerous positive reviews for IFE and Stephen, to be more precise, during my research for reputable international movers. I emailed Stephen for an interview and he speedily responded with an interview time and two client referrals. Here is what I learned:

IFE is based in Florida, but they have a partnership with Catalina and her company *Ecuador Movers*, which means you have someone in North America and in Ecuador to manage your move.

As a customer, you are provided support throughout your shipping process. Catalina is bi-lingual and will actually meet you in Guayaquil to help observe the inspection of your container. Stephen has vast personal experience undergoing no fewer than eight international moves. Not only does he understand the rules and regs, he understands what you go through. Catalina, born and raised in Ecuador, has vast experience dealing with Ecuadorian bureaucracy that would unlikely be achieved by a non-national.

SHIPPING & GAY COUPLES

I asked Stephen Aron from IFE, "What special consideration might gay couples face in regard to shipping a container?"

"I looked into it, and am told since gay marriage is not yet recognized in Ecuador, gay couples may not import their things in the same container. However, with heterosexual couples, only one person is allowed to be the importer, so the only obstacle to a gay couple shipping their things together would be the 200kg clothing allowance. They would not be permitted the allowance for two. Also, all of the boxes would have to be in the name of the importer. The clothes, shoes, and other belongings would have to be in a size similar to the importers personal measurements."
~ Stephen Aron

---

[28] http://www.ifeonline.com/page/ocean-freight

A look at the IFE website will lead you to the observation that their focus is on commercial moves (i.e. shipping planes). Stephen said he began shipping individuals to Ecuador after he was approached by someone online three years ago who couldn't find a reputable mover. Stephen understood his predicament and decided to help the fellow out. The services offered by IFE spread like wildfire through the expat world. Since then, he has moved well over a hundred families to Ecuador.

I also asked for a quote from Oklahoma City to Salinas, Ecuador to get an idea of their pricing and process. This was his response:

"Hi Shannon, we can offer $5,475.00 for a 20ft container 1,172 cu ft and $6,195.00 for a 40ftHC 2,669 cu ft positioned in Oklahoma City 73116 to Guayaquil including the Maersk handling charges in Guayaquil. This price does not include US Homeland Security checks on export cargo which, although are unlikely at most ports, are always possible and these are charged to the customer at cost.

The trucker allows two hours to load, after that it's $85.00 per hour driver detention. Insurance, if required, is available at $1.25/$100.00 for loss $1.75/$100.00 for loss or nondelivery and $2.25/$100.00 for loss, nondelivery or damage, so $10,000.00 coverage costs between $125.00 and $225.00, depending upon the selection, from load point to Salinas in Ecuador.

The costs from arrival to Guayaquil to unloading and delivery into your new residence (not including unpacking) are $3,510.00. The only cost in Ecuador that is not included in this bid is storage in Guayaquil if you take more than 12 days from arrival to return the empty container back to Maersk. There is a container deposit guarantee of $500.00 for a 20ft and $1,000.00 for a 40ft paid to Maersk and returned once they get their empty container back. If you exceed the 12 days, then they deduct the cost from your guarantee.

Although, I have separated the Ecuador charges, you can pay everything except the guarantee in the US or Ecuador, or split it as you'd like between the two countries.

Your Oklahoma goods can be shipped rail to LA, but rail can be tough on cargo and LA almost always stops containers for a customs exam, so I have quoted you with a truck from your residence to Houston. Then, it is a weekly service with a 24 day transit-time to Guayaquil.

I am attaching a sample packing list along with some packing tips and an extract from Ecuador customs.

We are happy to answer any questions you may have about the process and please let me know if the quote isn't completely clear to you."
~ Stephen Aron, International Freight Experts, Inc.
info@ifeonline.com

TIP

"Ecuador will seize your cargo if you don't follow procedure correctly. People joke you can get away with anything by greasing the process with money, but that simply isn't true."
~ Stephen Aron
International Freight Experts

ECUADOR MOVERS

Ecuador Movers came up a lot during my research and interviews. Catalina has numerous fans that express their thanks for her services across the internet. IFE (mentioned above) uses *Ecuador Movers* exclusively on the Ecuadorian side of things. At the writing of this book, the website was in construction. It will eventually be:
ecuadormovers.com
You can always email her at:
caty@ecuadormovers.com

OCEAN STAR INTERNATIONAL, INC.

While this mover maintains an A rating with the BBB and has been mentioned in Mover Mag and USA Today as one of the best moderately priced movers in the States, I cannot conclude that they would be the best mover due to some hellish stories I have read from their customers.[29] The short of it was, the client was guaranteed

---

[29] Read the full experience: http://bit.ly/movescam

a lowball rate, then after all of their worldly possessions were gathered and across the globe, Ocean Star doubled their fee and held the belongings ransom. "Come get your stuff or pay up" was how they treated their customers.

REINER OVERSEAS MOVERS

I have read good things about Reiner in regard to international shipping, but have heard nothing specific about the quality of their services in regard to Ecuador. I contacted them for a ballpark quote and here was their response:

"Did a ball park, 20 ft. 5000# lbs and came up with $9000.00 approx. including normal packing/loading, trucking the container from Oklahoma City to Houston for loading, ocean to Ecuador, customs clearance, and delivery to doorSalinas, Ecuador, unloading and unpacking, and same day debris removal. Excludes the port fees, from $1400.00 to 1700.00 and insurance, based on 2.50% of the declared value.

When you are ready for a free survey, let me know. I move lots of folks there, moving one of their Consul from Chicago at the end of the month."

Cesar Castro
Rainier Overseas Movers[30]
Director International Marketing

Container Experiences

Deana dropped $11k to ship a 40 foot container weighing 10,000 pounds from South Dakota, USA to Cuenca, Ecuador. She shares, *"I had an inventory list that was so specific, it was pages long. I believe it made a huge difference. There were no problems on the inspection because every box had a list of exactly what was in it. The inspector dug into the box, picked something up and found it on the inventory."*

Tomas shipped a 20 foot container from Miami to Cuenca for $7,700. The fee included insurance, storage, and local unloading.

"We used Stephen Aron of IFE for the US portion and Catalina with Ecuador Movers in Cuenca for the Ecuador side. We were very satisfied with both parties."

Dave shipped his container from Long Beach and unfortunately, ran into many snags. He spent $10,000 for

---

[30] http://bit.ly/rainierEC

door to door service 3 1/2 years ago. See his experience below:

"We used **Relocation Services of Ecuador** and had some serious problems. The container was not weighed in Long Beach, CA prior to shipping. The weight was a guess and when it arrived in Ecuador, it was weighed and they wanted to know when we added a car. There wasn't a car but a weight discrepancy of 4000 lbs. So it was dismantled in Guayaquil and many items were broken and/or stolen. Relocation Services promised us Customs clearance in Cuenca, and they said they sent someone to Guayaquil to supervise the ransack but he didn't show up. Then we had to clear Customs in Cuenca anyway. Our insurance was invalid after the initial opening of the container. The price was OK but the service sucked."

Clare Nowland reported:

"My husband and I shipped 1/2 container (20 ft) door-to-door from New Jersey to Cuenca in June, 2014. **All States** handled the US portion of the move, and **INSA** the shipping to Ecuador. We paid about $1400 in storage fees, as our things were stored in Guayaquil for 2 months while we awaited our visas. But many of our tools and electronics were stolen; and a lot of glassware, one TV and the vacuum were broken. Even the Rubbermaid storage tubs were cracked and split, like they had been flung from a truck or container into the storage unit. Insurance is not available for a shared container which is opened and loaded into temporary storage, so we lost another $1400 in personal property. The initial cost

for our shipment was about $3700. With storage, the total was $5000 for the 1/2 container. Our significant losses, most likely occurred when the container was opened."

Diane Bublack reported:

"Our container arrived at 2am and the inspection was quick and easy (we had very detailed and accurate lists as advised to us by Catalina, Ecuador Movers), but at our house the movers couldn't open the container because they couldn't get the metal covering that Customs used to re-seal the container over the back. Catalina said it's not my problem, it's there at your house. We had to pay the drivers extra $35-40 because they were out past a certain hour. Catalina said she would reimburse us but never did. She did give us good advice to buy a padlock and seal our container. We were the only ones with the key, so it was left alone until our inspection, then we resealed it directly thereafter. We had no issues with theft because of this."

Mike and Anna Maria Lentin Report:

"My wife & I would like to recommend strongly the services of Catalina Bermudez, owner/operator of Ecuador Movers. We hired Ms. Bermudez to move our entire household from a small town 400 miles north of Vancouver, Canada.

Our container arrived to the house one minute early and Ms. Bermudez phoned us immediately upon arrival. She arranged for the container to leave the Port of Vancouver a few days later. It arrived in Guayaquil 15 *days thereafter, & she brought it to Cuenca 2 days later for the obligatory Customs inspection. The inspection went smoothly & she delivered the container to our Cuenca condo that afternoon with a team of six men who unloaded all our furniture. Out of 124 boxes nothing was broken, damaged, or missing.*

Ms. Bermudez billed us the exact amount she had quoted. She also worked with our lawyer in Cuenca to ensure we gained our residency visa in time to avoid any duties.

She always answered our e-mails within 24 hours, & displayed great calm & professionalism.

To all Americans & Canadians planning the move to Ecuador, we very strongly recommend obtaining the services of Ms. Catalina Bermudez of Ecuador Movers (caty@ecuadormovers.com)."

DOCUMENTATION

The most important part of your shipping process is: "pack list, pack list, pack list." Every person interviewed (professional exporter or expat) stressed the importance of the pack list, and how it was the critical component of their move. It must be 100% accurate, ordered sequentially, thorough, and all boxes must be labeled correctly. Any discrepancy will delay your container. Each day your shipment is delayed incurs a $100 storage fee. You can see how spending extra time to make sure the lists are completely accurate before you send the container is time well spent!

AVOIDING SCAMMERS

The moving company:

☐ Should not ask for cash deposits before moving your items,

☐ Should have a physical address near your area, not a P.O. box,

☐ Should be licensed and insured,

☐ Should be a member of BBB (US side), and American Moving and Storage Association (AMSA),

☐ Should conduct an in-home evaluation for an accurate estimate, or require a detailed inventory list.,

☐ Be wary of low-ball prices,

```
┌─────────────────────────────────┐
│             TIP                 │
├─────────────────────────────────┤
```

In this instance, good karma is earned by abiding by the importing regulations, not by helping fellow expats ship in their personal merchandise.

You're playing with fire by adding a friend's most recent purchases on Amazon or other retailer to your container. You are required to prove that all belongings in your container are for your exclusive use. If you have unopened products from Amazon or products that were incorrectly added to your list (because favors are usually last minute), your container will be delayed. You will pay and your friendship may be tested. Don't play with fire, *just say no*!

See the end of this chapter for a moving checklist

SHIPPING YOUR CAR

The internet is packed with information about how to ship your car, what documents are needed, the taxes required, and rules about the procedure. I'm here to tell you that you cannot ship a car into Ecuador! Unfortunately, the rules have changed time and time again and right now the rule is a hard *NO*. In the past, expats were permitted to ship a car tax-free along with their household goods just like Ecuadorians who return after living abroad

SELLING YOUR CAR

Sell your car and pocket the cash for the big move. You're gonna need it if you hope to have a car in Ecuador!

Deciding whether to buy a car in Ecuador can be tricky. The first time I moved abroad, I thought I would foot it everywhere. I'm apparently not as bad-ass as I thought. I was whining about not having wheels and within one week, I was looking on Craigslist for used beaters for sale.

You can easily sell your car a variety of ways: through Craigslist, the Autotrader, a used car dealer, or my favorite option, through Carmax. I have sold two cars to Carmax and really appreciate their quick and honest service. It was particularly helpful when my car was not fully paid off, because they made the process so simple.

I walked in and asked for a quote for them to buy my car. After about 25 minutes, their technicians had finished a review of my car and I was handed a printed guaranteed offer. I compared it to Kelly Blue Book, Autotrader, and Craigslist equivalents.

Sure, I would miss out on a few hundred bucks but selling with Carmax was easy, convenient, and I could decide what day to give up my baby. So, I returned to Carmax the day before my flight, handed the sales team the guaranteed offer (good for one week) and asked to complete the sale.

Twenty minutes later, I walked out the door with a check! (*I also really appreciate purchasing cars with them, but that doesn't apply here, just thought I would share.*)

I have also sold and bought with Craigslist and the Autotrader. But after using them all, I really prefer Carmax because I don't have to worry about the individual I'm going to meet (at my house or some public lot), and there isn't the awkward haggling process. That to me, plus the fact I could keep the car until just before I left, was worth the difference in price.

SERVICES & RESOURCES

There are services out there that can help facilitate your entire relocation process. Everyone has a different set of variables, so I can't say all-inclusively what will work best for you. I can tell you what they do, the services they provide, and share with you stories from their clients.

GRINGO TREE

Gringotree.com proves to be an excellent resource for expats pondering the move abroad. They host an active expat community whose responses surpass any expectations I've held for online forums. The tone is also one of the most inviting that I have come across.

GRINGO POST

Gringopost.com is another commonly utilized resource for expats in Cuenca. It has a fairly active forum with expats rattling off questions like a pin-ball machine.

COASTAL NEWSLETTER

There is a new resource that is rapidly growing for those who are beach bound. A newsletter and growing community can be found at: http://bit.ly/salinasnewsletter

EcuaAssist

Excellent services for the expat

EcuaAssist[31] helps expats with all of their legal needs: visas, real estate contracts, title searches, legal services, estate management, will creation, incorporating businesses, and business guidance.

One great thing about EcuaAssist is they have translated all of the laws and contracts an expat may need into English. That way, you don't follow your lawyers words with blind faith, but can read them in English word for word.

I had the pleasure of interviewing one of the owners, and ten year veteran lawyer, Dr. Marcos Chiluisa. He shared, "Being an expat myself, I know how it feels. I understand what my clients are going through." (Dr. Chiluisa is originally from Venezuela, but has lived and worked in Ecuador for the last

15 years). Marcos really knows his stuff, speaks fluent English, is very patient, and serves the community through monthly legal seminars and occasionally contributes articles for the expat community.

His customers Bev & James Peterson had this to say about Maros and EcuaAssist:

"Marcos is sensitive, caring and detail minded. He knows how to identify with a person who wants to get a visa because he himself experienced that when he was a kid. His family had a huge struggle with it. He understands how lost you can feel at first. He is a bit more dedicated towards making sure his clients are getting every need met because he comes at it from a personal perspective.

We used EcuaAssist for all of our visas, cedulas, and censos. We couldn't be happier with the service and would give the highest recommendation.

We chose to go to Cuenca for our cedulas because we hadn't been yet and wanted to make it out there. They really made it easy. Kelsy (EcuaAssist) met us at the bed and breakfast in Cuenca and walked us through the process to get our cedulas. We were pretty much hand-held desk by desk for two hours. She set it all up, and never left our side, making it very easy for us. We had all of the paperwork we needed. We can't say

---

[31] http://bit.ly/EcuaAssist

enough about the positiveness of this. It was a wonderful welcome to Ecuador.

Marcos gave us his personal cell number and if anything needed to be rescheduled, he would let us know. We were never inconvenienced. If you want to be careful with your budget and time, he would be great to work with."

Dana Visa Specialists
agua_plata@hotmail.com

Along the coast, there were two consistently high performing visa services: EcuaAssist (they have a coastal office in addition to their Cuenca office) and visa specialist Dana Cameron based out of Guayaquil. Dana charges $500 for a resident visa and $75 for a cedula. Her fee includes translations.

EXPAT EXPERIENCE

I started the immigration process with Maite, she was able to get my visa after no fewer than 10 trips to Cuenca. I wish I would have known that there is nothing superior about going to Cuenca, and that Guayaquil would have worked just fine. Our multiple 10 hour bus journey each way was tiresome and expensive.

Maite went on vacation in the middle of our immigration, and container import process. She placed us in the hands of Catalina Bermuda and said not to worry. Things seemed to get very expensive when Catalina got involved. Most of the time if you do things the right way, you don't have $100 under the table fees here and there. That happened more often with Catalina. Other expats raved about them both, but our experience with Dana's service in Guayaquil was far superior. Not even comparable. She knew her stuff and all of the staff, many of whom she taught in college. This made it easier to get past small hangups.
~ Diane Bublack, expat from West Virgina

ELECTRONICS & TECHY TIPS

Decide which electronics you will need in EC and pack them. Keep in mind that house construction utilizes cement walls so wifi signals, on average, don't reach beyond one - two rooms. I use a booster[32] that I plug in at the top of the stairs. The booster catches the wifi signal from my combo cable modem/wifi router and boosts the signal to the rest of the upper level. Since I'm on the verge of being a tech geek (I'm not savvy enough for the full title), I wanted to have access to the internet in each room of the house.

If you are moving to an area serviced by a cable provider, it is a good idea to bring your own cable modem/wifi router.[33] This way you don't have to rent one from the cable company and can bring up-to-date hardware avoiding unnecessary slowing or glitches caused by older electronics. It can be tricky in Ecuador because DSL is still wildly used which requires a

---

[32] A device that picks up the wireless signal and repeats it (increasing the strength) http://bit.ly/boosteral

[33] A good wifi/modem combo unit: http://bit.ly/modemwifi

different type of modem, so make sure and check if there is cable service where you plan to land. With the humidity in coastal EC, the life expectancy for electronics is halved at best! Even with a de-humidifier, it is difficult to keep the water-filled air from rusting and destroying gadgets.

If you enjoy reading print books and magazines, the bad news is it will be more difficult to get your hands on English materials. There are a few good book stores in Cuenca and scattered across other touristy and expat-populated regions, but you certainly will be without your local Barnes N' Nobles and easy Amazon delivery. Electronic Readers are the most convenient option. Sure, you can't smell the book or see how far you are by gauging the remaining thickness. You can, however, shop in the Nook, Kindle, and iBook store

in addition to your library's free ebook download venue from the hammock in your villa, instantly downloading your next reading pleasure.

TIP

If you're an avid reader, one of the best things you can do before leaving is make sure you take a valid local library card with you to EC. This way, you will have access to their entire eBook library for free!

Test out the system before you leave and if you have any trouble, have a librarian teach you the ways of the library eBook before your departure! An eReader that can download apps is required.

OTHER ELECTRONICS:
- Laptop
- iPad
- Up-to-date smartphone *(who knows when you will be able to buy a new one)*
- Mobile speakers[34]

---

[34] Here is a link to an excellent waterproof bluetooth speaker: http://bit.ly/h20speakers

- Apple Tv[35] or Chrome for Windows users.
- Waterproof case[36] for your phone (for those refreshing downpours on your beach walks).
- External hard drive[37] to back up all of the amazing photos you will take.
- *Power surge protector*- you can pick this up in EC but make sure you use it. Lightening strikes have literally blown up appliances here.
- *Thumb/Flash drive* to take documents from your computer to be printed at a *Copia* store.
- *Video* camera and waterproof camera[38] with extra batteries *(what good is a camera if the battery is dead?)*.
- Nice pair of *headphones* with a mic for Skype.

- UPS (Uninterrupted Power Supply)[39] is a $40-$150 device that allows you to have uninterrupted power (by utilizing battery power) when you lose electricity in a storm. It has plugs and looks like a power surge protector on one side, and the other side harbors batteries. It stores energy while electricity is available, then when the power goes out, you have about 1.5-2 hours of battery life. *(Great for those telecommuters that need to keep the cable modem on.)*
- 140W adapter[40] for your car (plug your computer in while on long road trips).

---

[35] a device that connects to your TV's HDMI input and allows you to sign into your Netflix and Hulu accounts, rent off of iTunes, and access and Apple computer music and video library right on your HD TV. Here is a link: http://bit.ly/appletv03

[36] The best waterproof case for iPhones is made by LifeProof: http://bit.ly/lfeprof

[37] An easy to use, speedy 1T back up drive is made by Lacie: http://bit.ly/lacie1T

[38] This video camera is best for rugged outdoor adventures: http://bit.ly/goproexpat

[39] http://bit.ly/powersupplyoutage

[40] This is the one I have: http://bit.ly/140Wadapter

STREAMING MUSIC AND VIDEO

The sun goes down around 6:20pm year-round in Ecuador. With extra time on your hands in the evening, movie nights can be a great treat!

If you are accustomed to Pandora, Hulu, Instant Movies on Amazon, or Crackle, I have good news and bad news for you. At the time of my writing, they do not have licensing for Ecuador. The good news is you can download a free program to "bounce" your IP address. In laymen terms, the program will play hide-and-seek with the numbers that report to the internet gods where the connection is coming from.

The program that I use is called Hotspot Shield.[41] There are numerous programs, but not all are free. You can listen to all the music you want. Another option for music streaming is Spotify which has no restrictions to function in Ecuador.

Netflix works just fine in Ecuador but will not hold the identical directory as the Netflix in the States. Since there is no DVD subscription, they offer more instant watch options. While the catalog is larger, they take away some instant watches that are available in the United States. I'm guessing the variance relates to the show's copyright restrictions.

If you are a movie freak and would love to host movie night at your house or in your backyard consider getting a portable screen and projector. Since it's dark so early, it would be a great way to spend some quality time with your neighbors!

BEST APPS FOR EXPATS

Jump into the app store and be immediately lost, intimidated, and frustrated. How do you find quality apps that will suit you? The best apps I've discovered have been mostly by word of mouth. As

---

[41] To review or download this free program go to: http://bit.ly/ipbouncer

an expat who is a former Apple employee and a total Mac geek, let me share with you my favorite apps specifically with the expat in mind.

Skype

Probably, the most used and most valuable app for expats. This is a must have app. So you have downloaded Skype on your computer. Once you have a smart phone or tablet, download the free app and sign in.

I highly recommend making two purchases on Skype: an unlimited calling subscription (premium plan $60 a year) and a personalized phone number (another $60 a year). I purchased the subscription that allows unlimited calling to landlines and cell phones in the United States. I paid around $3 a month. Rates constantly change with different promos, but typically Skype rewards you for paying for the entire year in advance. The other purchase was just as important. If you don't purchase a number then businesses,

family, and friends can't call you. While you can call them anytime you want, they will see a different number each time and not know it's you. You can choose your area code when you purchase a number.

I take Skype with me everywhere I can get cell service on my iPhone app. That way, I can make a call to loved ones or for business back to the States. If anyone needs to reach me and I have Skype logged in on my phone, it will ring!

There are competing apps that offer similar phone service such as Vonage, magicJack, and TextPlus. Skype has been at it the longest, has a proven track record, and adds video conferencing and instant message features. The second most popular internet phone service is magicJack.

Viber

Another free talk and text app that is growing in popularity, but unlike Skype it doesn't require invitation to connect to others. It automatically incorporates your phone book.

The biggest drawback is those who you wish to communicate with must also be on Viber.

WhatsApp

In case you have been under a rock for the last 5-7 years, texting is practically required to keep in touch with people. I'm certain you know people who refuse to answer their phone, but will quickly reply to a text. International text messages get pricey if you don't know about great apps like WhatsApp.

Build a free account and text away! The drawback is the person whom you wish to text needs to be a WhatsApp user. This, however, is an extremely common and well established app, so it shouldn't pose much of a problem. The app is also a great way to send pictures without getting charged fees!

An alternative app that doesn't require your text-ees to have the same app is TextPlus. With TextPlus, you can choose a phone number (including the area code), and that number will be your texting number.

You can send and receive texts on said number for free!

Voxer

"Breaker Breaker, Foxtrotter's on the move." I loved walkie-talkies as a kid. This app allows you to talk to other people just like you are both on walkie-talkies, or Nextels, except you aren't restricted to a 200 foot range. You can walkie-talkie with someone in Africa if they have the app and a cellular signal.

If you hate text messaging, you'll love this. If the second you get behind the wheel you need to text everyone, talk into the phone instead, and they will get your walkie message.

The downside of this app is the same as WhatsApp. The other user must also have the app downloaded, but they don't have to be logged in to receive the message. The app will notify them a new message is waiting to be heard. In order to talk back and forth in real time, both parties need to have the app open.

Google Voice

Google Voice allows the user to port their phone number to Google Voice and then forward it to a second number. Currently, they do not allow forwarding to an international number, but you can forward it to your Skype number!

It gets a little confusing, but basically you can tell Google Voice, via the set up on its website, which contacts you want to call and which of your phone numbers to use (i.e. the Skype number you purchased) then Google Voice will use wifi to make the call.

Other benefits include: multiple number call forwarding, a wide variety of voicemail options (different voicemail messages depending on the number dialed), an excellent spam call filtering, and voicemail transcripts via your email!

You must set up Google Voice from the States. It will not allow you to do so once on ground in Ecuador. To learn more about how Skype and Google Voice can integrate see: http://bit.ly/skypegv

XE Currency

This app is exactly what it sounds like, a currency converter. While Ecuador uses the dollar, it's nice to have in case you decide to visit neighboring Peru or Colombia.

Google Translate

A translator app every expat should have in their arsenal is Google Translate. Even if you are not in the smart phone arena, make sure and take advantage of Google Translate on your computer. The biggest drawback of the app is that it requires cellular service or wifi to work. If you are struggling with the same word, however, it remember previous translation requests.

Word Lense

This app was recently acquired by Google. You open the app and click record on a sign you wish to translate. Word Lense instantly translates anything in print using your built-in video camera in real time!

TripIt

As an avid traveler, I love this app! It's the ultimate travel organization resource. Sometimes I book my airfare, hotels/ hostels, and rental cars months out while other times only days ahead.

After I downloaded TripIt, created an account, and authorized it to access my email, I no longer needed to worry about printing or organizing my confirmation emails. I used to search my email for these confirmation codes, reservation codes, etc. Now, because TripIt recognizes when I receive an email confirmation, it automatically adds the information to the app!

TripIt also allows you to create trips. I recently returned from a three month trip to South America. I was able to separate all of my reservations by creating multiple trips, each one defined by a span of dates: Machu Picchu trip, Ecuador trip, Wedding Trip, and Honeymoon trip. It was so great to see all of my complex plans organized so clearly without an ounce of effort on my part.

After I set the dates, any new confirmations for those dates automatically got added to the corresponding trip. I was able to access my trip plans on my iPad, iPhone, or any computer by going to Tripit.com. How great is that?

TripAdvisor

This app is great if you are on the move. My wife and I take last-minute road trips frequently, and TripAdvisor really helps us find hotels, attractions, and outdoor activities. I love the "near me" option. It's a great *save me* app when I don't do my homework! The downside is it's super slow. The lag factor is really annoying, but if you use it in a restaurant or hotel with wifi, it's not *as* bad as on 3 or 4G.

Convert Units

This is really only needed if you are from the US. Since the United States is hell bent on being different, we don't know: what a price per kilo gets us, if we are speeding at 50 kph, how much space is $1000m^2$, or how large is 2 hectares of land. Until you learn these new measurements, an app like Convert Units is very helpful.

Kindle

Everyone has heard about the Kindle. What you might not have heard is how hard it is to find books written in English in Ecuador. Unless you are in Cuenca or other large expat community, it can be very difficult. So even though I prefer a book in my hand over a screen, I have completely sold out to the Kindle App. It's nice to have all my books in my skinny iPad and iPhone.

Kindle just added *Kindle Unlimited* which offers unlimited reading for one monthly fee of $9.99. Interestingly enough, it was launched just a few short months after two other companies offered monthly subscriptions for unlimited reading.

I chose the Kindle App as my primary reader over iBooks and the Nook because as an Amazon derivative, it is often $2 or $3 cheaper than the Barnes N' Noble's Nook. All three programs have similar interfaces, so no deciding factor there. The Kindle has more inventory than any other book app. Even though I am a Mac geek, I don't see any Apple oohs and awwws like I usually do regarding their reader. I miss Steve Jobs...

Overdrive

Use your library card and download free eBooks to *Overdrive* for your reading pleasure. Thousands of libraries use Overdrive, check to see if yours does. Why buy books when you can get them for free! If you don't have a library card, get one before you leave. All you need is a photo ID with a local address or an ID and a piece of mail with a local address. It's a no brainer! You will even have access to free magazines and newspapers.

Oyster

If you read so much that the library offerings won't cut it and you would prefer a book over watching a movie on Netflix, then you may want to consider a subscription with the book version of Netflix, Oyster. With one monthly rate of $9.95, you can read unlimited books anytime, anywhere! They have a free trial, so check them out if it sounds up your alley.

Dropbox

Dropbox has been around the block many times now and is still the cloud service leader. There are numerous competitors these days: Onedrive, ShareFile, CX, Cloudme, TeamDrive, Egnyte, Huddle, Cubby, Syncplicity, Box, Amazon Cloud Drive, Wuala, SugarSync, and SpiderOak to name a few. I'm sure that many are just as good as Dropbox.

I have stuck with DB because it has never failed me, and that kind of consistency with my key documents is important. They have tried to spruce things up by adding a photo loader that launches anytime a camera is hooked up to your computer, but I don't use that feature.

A free subscription caps at 2 GB which is plenty for thousands of documents. I have many of my documents and manuscripts backed up for my publishing business on Dropbox. I recently reached my limit when I started to receive video footage from other authors via Dropbox. Now I pay $9.99 a month for 100GB of cloud service. I primarily use an external drive for my video production company, and a second external hard drive to back up my entire computer (including my pictures and video content).

Don't be caught without a backup in the States or in Ecuador. You cannot recreate the memories captured in your thousands of pictures. I'm also sure you don't want to re-create that presentation for work or rebuild your music collection.

In Ecuador, your computer liability increases. The humidity is like kryptonite to your hard drive, sand is the devil, and you can be sure that both will be in your computer if you live near the beach. Even in Cuenca, it can get wet with the persistent cloud cover and rain.

Flickr

With Flickr, everyone is given 1000 gigs (1TB) for storage of photos for free. That's roughly 500,000 photos (the figure varies greatly depending on your resolution). You can even set it up to automatically save photos that you are taking on your smart phone instantly! Flickr can be used as an excellent online backup resource so you don't lose those priceless experiences so meticulously captured on camera! Plus you can easily share albums with friends via email or Facebook. Speaking of Facebook...

Facebook

While you may not have been a "Facebooker" in the past, once you live in a different country you may re-think your stance. Facebook provides a way to stay connected and informed in your loved ones' lives. You can see pictures from their trips, watch their children grow up, and comment on each adorable photo, making a virtual appearance in their lives when a physical one isn't possible. You can also share your adventures in Ecuador.

I know from experience that people love seeing new exotic places. After seeing some of your gorgeous photos, they might be compelled to plan a trip to visit you!

Photocard

The post office system in Ecuador is flawed at best. Packages arriving empty is not uncommon. Postcards usually make it to the States but take 4-8 weeks! Photocard is a cool app that lets you assign a picture you have taken on your iPhone/ iPad as the postcard cover, then allows you to write a message in a variety of fonts and sizes. It even has stickers so you can decorate the card. Once completed, you purchase one credit for $2.99 to have it printed and put into the US mail that day! Two to three days later, your grandkids, buddies, parents, or clients will be surprised with a fun, personal, and customized card from you!

Weather Underground

I enjoy the interface of this weather app on the iPhone. One standout is it's hyper local specific reports. It utilizes social interaction to assure the accuracy from one neighborhood to the next. Other pluses: it's incredibly user friendly, gorgeous displays for forecasts, wind speed, precipitation, sunrise/sunset data, and has an easy to use radar feature. You can also easily add different cities around the world to the app so you can call up your family and ask them how the snow storm is coming along.

Google Maps / WAZE

Both of these apps are great GPS resources. I personally have utilized Google Maps as my primary routing app. There was only one instance living in Costa Rica where Google Maps didn't have the roads I needed to reach my destination (in this instance, Rio Celeste). Surprisingly enough, Mapquest did have the roads in question. My adventures in Ecuador were 100% satisfied by Google Maps.

WAZE is a fun to use GPS app that also has social data such as eyewitness accident information, police checkpoints, and more. It allows you as the user to add up-to-date information about an accident you passed, a broken down vehicle, or a cop with a radar gun locked and loaded! So if you're stuck in traffic, open up WAZE and see what the holdup is, or better yet, check WAZE before you commit to a route.

Juice Defender Plus

Run this app to extend battery life on Andriod-operated smart phones. I could say something snide like, "Apple doesn't need an app like this because of their superiority," but now that would be rude!

For those of you who scoff at how technology can help you enjoy an international life with the remarks, "I moved here to get away from all of that." This section was clearly not for you. To each their own, right?

SET UP YOUR COMMUNICATION SYSTEM

UNLOCK YOUR PHONE

Almost all phones purchased in North America are locked by their original carrier so only sim cards provided by the carrier will function with the phone. Make certain you can unlock the phone for use in Ecuador. Otherwise, the phone is no good to you as an expat.

First determine if you are under contract with your service provider. If you are, you must either finish your term or pay a steep early cancellation fee. After your contract has expired or terminated and you have a zero balance on your account including your phone, you are legally entitled to an unlocked phone.

Each carrier handles the unlock differently. AT&T has a customer service department that is "suppose to" unlock your phone after receiving a written request and the phone's IMEI number. I tried this route numerous times for my iPhone with no response. I found that using $10 and a third party service was the way to go. There are numerous services that do an excellent job providing you with a factory unlock (i.e. no hacking) within 24 hours. One that I have used successfully numerous times is: http://bit.ly/unlckphone

T-Mobile's policy is if there is no balance remaining on the purchase of your phone, they will unlock it. Simply dial 611 which directs you to their customer service. Tell them you are going on a trip abroad and need the phone unlocked. It may take them up to 48 hours to complete the unlock.

If you have a phone with Verizon, Sprint, MetroPCS, Cricket, or U.S. Celluar, then it's time to go shopping because they are CDMA phones and will not work in most of Ecuador. CNT has a very small network for CDMA service, but it's basically a joke. I believe it's best to just leave it behind in the States.

Ecuador is in conjunction with the rest of the world on the GSM network. If this is all Greek to you, pretend that GSM is on one radio station and CDMA is on another but the dial is broken. The US decided to be different (shocker right?) opting for the CDMA network when it was new and exciting. So you can put your old phone next to your yardstick on your way out of the country.

BANDWIDTH

Make sure your phone supports the GSM-850 bandwidth. Ecuador uses this bandwidth exclusively. You can go to www.phonearena.com and enter in your phone to find out which frequencies it supports.

SKYPE

Features:
- ☑ Skype to Skype calling
- ☑ International calls
- ☑ Call waiting
- ☑ Video
- ☑ Messaging
- ☑ Sharing
- ☑ Personalized number
- ☑ Smart phone app

If you are not already a Skype user then go to www.skype.com and create a new account. Take care to remember your user name so you can give it to your loved ones. After you create an account, make sure all of the people that you wish to "Skype" have also created accounts. Make a few trial runs to work out the bumps. Call up your mom, daughter, son, or BFF and ask them to login. Stay on the phone in case they encounter "technical difficulty." Test video conferencing, instant messaging, voice calls, and sending pictures or files over Skype. That way, when you're thousands of miles away, you will know how it works and the process required.

If you choose Skype as your main source of international communication, you will want to purchase a personalized phone number and subscription. See the **Communication** section in **After You Have Arrived** for more information.

TEXT MESSAGING

Texting has become a form of communication to keep in touch with our younger generation. In fact, there is a whole new language being created around texting. BRB... Ok, I'm back!

International texting gets pricey fast! There is a solution with a few excellent apps that allow you to text for free. *I use WhatsApp and TextPlus which I covered above in* **Best Apps For Expats**. Your Skype account will allow you to text but it will cost you. The amount is displayed in the lower right corner of the texting space. It usually ranges from 9-15 cents per message. You must add "Skype credit" before you can text.

magicJack

☑ International calls
☑ Call waiting
☑ Transfer your number
☑ Use a regular phone!
☑ Smart Phone app
☑ Caller ID

The most popular internet phone services are Skype and magicJack, hands down. If you prefer to use a wireless phone or even a wired phone at home, magicJack has some extraordinary gizmos so you don't have to take the call through your computer. Skype has come out with a few gadgets[42] recently to respond to the magicJack Plus.

MJ also has free call waiting! You are required to purchase the device that translates the cable-modem signal to a phone jack receiver. You will need a regular phone or computer to use the magicJack. You can either transfer your number or select a new one. They provide a 30 day free trial, but you are required to pay a subscription. If you decide to go with the magicJack, make sure and order the device before departure and bring a phone with you so you can take advantage of all the options.

DATA

Many people experience difficulty setting up their data services with their iPhone, iPad, or other smart device using EC service providers.

APN settings are settings in your phone that often need to be adjusted in order to assure your data plan functions correctly.

Once you have a sim card and are able to make calls, turn off the wifi and check to see if you can receive your email or search the web. If you can, then you don't need to make any adjustments to your APN settings. If you can't, then this is most likely the hurdle keeping you from connectivity. If you have no idea where the setting is located, Google "Where is the APN setting on a ____ phone?" See *below* for appropriate APN settings for each EC cellular provider.

---

[42] See some of the options ranging from $20-$100: http://bit.ly/skypephne

Movistar
Username: movistar
Password: movistar

Claro
Username: *(blank)*
Password: *(blank)*

CNT
Username: *(blank)*
Password: *(blank)*
APN name:
internet3gsp.alegro.net.ec

Moving Checklist

☐ Go to www.intlmovers.com and get quotes and companies that serve your two points of location

☐ Ask for recommendations from friends, expat forums, AREC, and read testimonials found in this chapter

☐ Double check with the BBB regarding the potential company

☐ Find out what the mover will do if an item is damaged in transit

☐ Obtain at least three estimates from various companies and compare their costs with their corresponding services and ratings

☐ Find out if the mover is registered with FMCSA. http://ai.fmcsa.dot.gov/hhg/Search.asp?ads=a

☐ Determine when and how your items will be picked up

☐ Acquire all contact information for the movers for each step of the process: before, during, and after the move

☐ Purchase insurance for your items

Moving Day

☐ If at all possible, be present to answer questions and oversee work

☐ Watch the inventory process and make sure the condition of your items is correctly documented because this list is used to calculate your taxes

☐ Keep your bill until you have all possessions in your new home and all claims are settled if applicable

☐ After the truck drives away, perform a final walk through so you don't forget anything

☐ Make sure the appropriate party has directions to your new home in Ecuador!

☐ If your contact info changes, update it with the movers and drivers

Delivery Day

☐ Be present to answer any questions, inventory the boxes, and direct traffic

☐Supervise unloading and unpacking (if applicable) of your goods

☐Make sure the inventory list reflects any damaged items before you sign any documents

☐Pay your driver or sign documents authorizing payment according to the terms of your agreement

• Reference the back of the book for **PACKING TIPS, INVENTORY PACK LIST, & ECUADOR'S CUSTOMS REGULATIONS**

After You Arrive

You have arrived after you step off the plane, through the jetway, and out the doors where the warm moist air greets you (in Guyaquil), or the cool dry wind zips across your face (Quito) welcoming you to Ecuadorian soil.

Bienvenido a Ecuador
"Welcome to Ecuador"

Welcome to your new life as an expat. Make sure to soak up this moment, celebrate it! Don't rush past it, you are no longer in a hurry. Settle into the rhythm of the country.

> **EXPAT EXPERIENCE**
>
> *"I felt like I belonged when I set foot here. I don't even feel belonged in a family reunion."*
> ~ Diane Bublack, expat from West Virginia

If you were unable to make an exploratory trip to explore the regions and secure housing, make sure to plan for at least a few weeks of exploration, and hotel/hostel stay while you find your rental. The last thing you want to do is jump into the first rental you see, since the region and your home will greatly affect your overall satisfaction with life in Ecuador. The more places you tour, the better suited your selected home will be.

FINDING A RENTAL

North Americans and Europeans are planners. We want to know exactly where we're going, how long we will be there, and exactly how much "there" will cost. This way of living doesn't completely jive with the culture of Ecuador. While it is possible to arrange your accommodations ahead of time and sign a lease for a year before you land, I highly discourage it. If you don't wish to spend the beginning of your trip looking at houses and regions then I suggest you take a separate "scouting" trip sometime before the actual move.

If you are hoping to land along the coast, be aware that the rental market is very fluid. Ecuadorians and gringos often visit for shorter spans of time which causes a large flux in inventory. In mountain regions like Cuenca, people are usually looking long term. Since the coast is seasonal, the prices double in the high season and triple during the holidays. For a high season rental (Christmas through Easter), try to make arrangements by August or September.

A scouting trip dedicated to hunting for rentals and exploring potential cities is a necessity! This is the best time to discover how close or far the grocery store is, and where the bus station or gas stations are. After you have viewed at least 8-10 homes, write down a list of must haves and wants to see which home suits you best. Assess the regions by using the W-A-S-P acronym discussed in the *Where in Ecuador is Your Haven* section.

PURCHASING A HOME

If you haven't yet, read the *Try Before You Pry* section before you proceed.

The first step is to gather referrals for an excellent attorney or broker making sure the referrals are from people who actually purchased property through him/her. Then set up an appointment and ask any and all questions you have about purchasing property after you have read this guide. If you are at all curious what USAID has to say about property rights in Ecuador read their pdf: http://bit.ly/USAIDec

Next, start searching for properties in your desired location. If you opt to have an agent assist you, know that there is very little enforcement regarding real estate regulations in place in Ecuador. That means, oftentimes people run around calling themselves an agent, but are not licensed and may have zero knowledge about the laws and market.

Ask what their commission is upfront and get it in writing. That way if it ever changes for any circumstances, you have it in black and white.

There is no such thing as an exclusive agent in Ecuador, so feel free to shop around and see which agent you like the best, and who shows you properties that are closer to your wish list and budget.

Once you have located a property or home to purchase, and your attorney has reviewed the title and given you the ok, you or your agent will present the buyer with a written offer and an earnest money deposit.

Two companies that I have interviewed and have spoken with their clients are:

Cuenca Area: Ecuador at Your Service (Ashley & Michel)

Coastal: RE/MAX Pioneer Realty[43] - Salinas, Ecuador (Amy Prisco)

TITLE/DEED

In Ecuador they don't have title insurance, it just doesn't exist. Which is why it's extremely important to know for sure who the owner(s) is.

A lot of the coastal land is communal, which means it isn't deeded. You will have to legalize the land first in order to get a dead.

---

[43] http://bit.ly/remaxamy

PURCHASING A PROPERTY

If you have constructed a home in the United States then you are familiar with the seemingly endless details that are required in order to make a quality home. Add to that, minimal regulation (unless in the historic districts), a language barrier, a confusing permit process, and Ecuadorian time and you have Ecuadorian construction! On the plus side, labor is very cheap and many materials are cheaper here (with a few exceptions).

There are numerous lots for sale. Peruse at a slow pace. Consider potential growth, access to public utilities, and infrastructure. Remember, many of the owners of those lots you are drooling over are selling them because they made a hasty purchase. Do your research, and live in the area where you are considering buying prior to purchasing. Purchasing a lot is a fairly quick process, selling one can take years.

When house or property hunting, take into account you are in a new culture. Business is conducted differently in Ecuador.

Ecuadorians aren't as clear and up front about pricing. Don't rush them to tell you the price, otherwise you will hear one you won't like. More often, locals prefer to do business with someone they know. Try to arrange a time when you can meet the seller, shake hands and get to know them a little bit. Developing a rapport can really affect their selling price. Asking them for the price upfront can startle them into a high number. If you warm them up with conversation, and a beer or coffee, you can knock off thousands of dollars!

TIP

"The most common trick I've seen in lot sales is when the seller shows an expat a larger property than is actually documented. It happens a lot on the coast of Ecuador. At EcuaAssit, we bring a GPS with us, take measurements, and use a boundary sign engineer to manage this problem."
~ Dr. Marcos Chiluisa
EcuaAssist

EXPAT EXPERIENCE

"There are always going to be frustrations when building new construction. Our frustrations were amplified by our builder basically walking away and leaving the construction to an Ecuadorean who spoke virtually no English. We hired a gringo intermediary, Gary, because we wanted U.S. quality construction and we wanted to be able to communicate without the fear of misunderstandings. This turned out to be the biggest hurdle that we encountered. Because of the lack of oversight, many things on our construction were done incorrectly. We moved into our home in October 2013 (three months later than the construction contract) and it is now March and we are still waiting for Gary and his 'crew' to fix the punch list items. We do not really anticipate ever seeing him again.

The positives about buying and building are you know the construction is new, you have no hidden scares in the walls, and for us, it is what we wanted. We chose our own cabinet maker, who is amazing. (Don Pedro Edison – La Libertad, Ecuador) Our allowance for the cabinets included only kitchen cabinets ($4,500). But our kitchen is relatively small, so we got two floor to ceiling wardrobes, master bath vanity, and the kitchen for just over $5,000."
~ Diane Bublack, expat from West Virginia

Lesson two, let's say you successfully secured a meeting with the owner. If you pull up in a fancy car, dressed to the nines, displaying fancy jewelry, you will have just tanked any chance at a low ball offer. Ecuadorians already think you, as a gringo, are rich. Now they are certain you are rich and the sky is the limit with their selling price.

TIP

"Although initial asking prices are almost always higher for gringos, a gringo with the right attitude, strategy, and patience can often negotiate a price just as low as any Ecuadorian. The key is to not be in a rush and get to know the people you are dealing with before you make any offers."
~ Ashley & Michel
EcuadoratYourService.com

As of May 22nd, 2014 any foreigner that buys property in Ecuador has to have an Ecuadorian tax ID number.[44] For those people who aren't planning on living in Ecuador immediately, like those on a week long buying trip, this is an inconvenient but not insurmountable hurdle.

---

[44] In Salinas, other cities initiated enforcement sooner, and I'm sure other are in the process of initiating enforcement

There is a way around it. Consult with your agent to find the necessary paperwork. The municipality is rejecting any new deeds that do not have Ecuadorian tax identification clearance.

BANK LOANS in Ecuador

Most expats who arrive with the intention of buying, arrive with cold hard cash in order to secure their Ecuadorian abode. For those of us who have "eggless-nests" options are slowly creeping our direction!

Foreigners do not currently qualify for home loans in Ecuador. However, if you buy directly from a new construction agent in an ongoing construction project, the construction company can provide you with a financing option.

There are also people who have secured personal loans from their banks located in their country of origin. It can be a long-shot, but if you have a good history and relationship with a smaller bank, sometimes they will go to bat for you.

OWNER-FINANCING

This is not a popular route, just yet. It's a bit of a long-shot. However, we are seeing a slow increase in owners willing to jump into this potential mess in order to secure a buyer.

There are a variety of different arrangements with owner-financing so make sure you are comfortable with your terms. Be careful to choose a structure that protects both the buyer and seller. This method is seen more frequently in Costa Rica, and I believe it's slowly trickling down to Ecuador.

REAL ESTATE AGENTS

There are licensure requirements in Ecuador in order to work as a Real Estate Agent, however, there is very little enforcement of said regulations. I recommend you ask from the start if they are licensed and where you can verify it. Also, make sure to learn what their fee is and get it in writing! Find out how many people are involved in a potential purchase. Is the real estate agent's friend who referred you getting a cut, the taxi driver who drove you to the appointment, the dog who saw you approaching the building and looked extra cute to draw you in? See if they are getting additional money from you on top of the agent's fees. To read more about the escrow process and fees read the *Purchasing a Home* section.

SQUATTERS

The last thing that any homeowner wants is a squatter in their house. In the United States, it's a health, safety, and financial hazard. In Ecuador, you're in danger of losing your property. *Listen up part-time expats!* Squatters have rights in EC. Land ownership functions differently in EC. You need to be aware of these rights.

If squatters occupy your "unoccupied" house and land and work for a period of time, they start to accrue property rights. Eventually, they can apply for its expropriation from the "absentee landlord." There have been instances in rural towns on foreign-owned land where a large organized group of squatters entered the land and created make-shift shelters. Due to their size, it was much harder to evict them.

What do you do if you find out a squatter is on your property? You must immediately file for an eviction order. If you catch it early and you can prove that, the procedure could be simple. However, the powers that be tend to favor the squatters.

When purchasing a house, take extra care to make sure signs of squatters are not present. If there is a caretaker of the property, make sure they really are a caretaker and not a squatter that may already have rights to the same property you seek to purchase. If you are concerned about squatters, film your property frequently so you have proof of improvements and changes demonstrating the property is not abandoned.

If you plan to leave for an extended period, make sure you have a caretaker on the property to keep squatters out. You can place an ad in the "Caretaker Gazette" or other house sitting sites (listed in the *How to Live for Free* section) for someone to house or pet sit your property. You provide the chores to be completed daily and the time span they will reside on your property.

In exchange for taking care of your property, they receive a free place to live! It's a win win! Create a written contract that each party signs so that he/she cannot become a squatter. In addition, have a neighbor or close friend that you trust keep an eye on the property, popping in to say hi, and check out the place every few months.

LOCAL BANKING

To open a local account or not to open a local account, *that* is the question… There are pros and cons to establishing a local banking solution. Most expats opt to utilize a local bank for monthly bills such as cell phone, cable, groceries (ATM card), and rent. All

things considered, opening an account opens doors for you.

Pros

• *Access to services*- You'll need a local account for many services. Some cell phone and internet providers require a bank account.
• *Replacement*-If you lose your bank card, it's easier to get replaced because it's in country.
• *Risk control*- Using your local card is also better for managing risk because you will never have large sums of money in said account.
• *Bill Pay*- You have many more bill pay options with local banks, which means less errands and less lines to wait in.
• *Street credit*- Drop that local card, yes, you are a local! Verified by an Ecuadorian bank!

Cons

• *Hassle* - Initial hassles setting up the account

- *Risk-* Whatever money you have in the account is not FDIC insured, and Ecuador banking is not super stable.

John, an expat from Toronto, Canada who also works in Ecuador, shares his opinion about local banking:

"My Canadian income stays in Canada and my Ecuadorian income gets used here. Taxes are paid to both countries but only on the income earned in each country.
Service charges are the issue as the Canadian banks charge $5.00 per transaction (at least that is what mine charges). Using ATM's is the best way to get cash. Since my pension is deposited into a Canadian bank that I have access to through ATMs, I don't need to have a bank here.

The only reason to open an account here would be to use the bank as a method of paying bills.

I opened an account at the same bank that my employer uses (I am an expat but I am working here for a few months.) in hopes it would make the process of cashing or depositing my cheque easier. It helps a little. I still need to show my passport to cash the cheque and access my money. The account is available through local ATM's but the daily limit is ridiculously low. Sending money back home is VERY expensive (5% of the amount being transferred, if it is over $1000.00, or $55 if less than $1000.00)."

Getting it Done

- Application (filled out during your meeting)
- Passport in hand
- Residence Card (Censo of registration from the Ministry of Foreign Affairs)
- Proof of address (copy of a utility bill less than 60 days old)
- Letter of recommendation (From someone who has an account at the bank you are applying at. They must sign it with their account number and cedula or passport number.)
- Deposit at least USD$300
- When in doubt, bring copies of everything.

SETTING UP UTILITIES

If you have rented your home, utilities are more than likely already set up for you. Don't expect them to be changed into your name. It is so difficult to change the account that most landlords don't even bother. Make sure that if the utilities are not included in your rent, you are given the account numbers, and corresponding account owners' names for the water and electric bills. That comes in handy when it's time to pay!

With the account information in hand, you can now pay most of your bills online (if you have a bank account), or at various banks with a small commission (about $0.50), or finally, at **Servipagos paypoints** (i.e. electric, water, and cable). Gas

---

TIP

"Electric bills must be paid during a neighborhood's five-day window and usually involve long waits in line. Houses with stores and restaurants, which is common, must pay two different electric bills at two different rates, one for the business and one for the residence. While online payment is an option, hardly anyone uses it because they must pay their water bill in person, which can be paid at the same time as their electric bill."
Kat Davis
http://bit.ly/katdavis

---

is as simple as switching out tanks! You can call a private gas company to come out and

replace your empty with a full for a few bucks!

INTERNET

Your internet provider is the only utility that is often placed in your name unless your landlord includes it in your rent. Grupo TVCable[45] serves much of Ecuador offering economic plans!

2.6 Mb:	$19.90
4.1 Mb:	$29.90
5.6 Mb:	$39.90
7.1 Mb:	$49.90
16.5 Mb:	$99.90
19 Mb:	$114.90

For those of you who aren't "mega" tech savvy, most starter plans in the US are in the 2 Megabyte range (speed) and will run you around $50. If you reference that to the prices above, you are well under half the price. I used to pay $60 for 4 megabytes in Costa Rica!

---

[45] http://www.grupotvcable.com.ec/grupo/internet

ETAPA Internet

ETAPA is a government-owned company that services Cuenca providing internet, telephone, and drinking water. Their plans start at 1.8 MB for $19.99 and top out at 10MB for $78 bucks.
http://www.etapa.net.ec

PuntoNet Internet

Another big hitter in the internet-world is PuntoNet with offices in: Guayaquil, Quito, Cuenca, Ambato, Ibarra, La Libertad, Loja, Machala, Manta, Portoviejo, Riobamba, Salinas, Tulcán, Santo Domingo, Quevedo, Latacunga, Babhoyo, Azogues, and El Coca. Their pricing is much like ETAPA with its start at 1.7 MB for $19.90 capping out at 5 MB for $49.90.
http://www.puntonet.ec

CentroNet Internet

CentroNet serves Cuenca by attaching an antenna to their client's house which then receives a wireless signal.

http://www.centronet.net.ec

CNT

Corporación Nacional de Telecomunicaciones (CNT) is another government-owned telecommunication company. Once again the rates aren't drastically different from the others starting at $18 for 2 MB and capping at $105 per month for 15 MB.
http://www.cnt.gob.ec

Cesacel

Cesacel is a small provider that serves: Santa Isabel, Girón, Nabón, San Fernando, Azogues, and Biblián. They also mount an antenna to your roof, specializing in areas that don't have other options, which explains their more expensive plans. For 700 Kbps you will owe $18.50, they top out at only 2 MB for $50.50 (over double what it costs from its' competitors).
http://www.cesacel.net.ec

LOCAL COMMUNICATION

LANDLINE

A few of the cable companies also offer phone service: TVCable, ETAPA, CNT, all have landline phone and internet packages.

These days many folks opt to use their cell phone as their home phone, or rely on Skype or magicJack for home phone capabilities. For others, they need to have a connection that isn't dependent on electricity and is more reliable in case of an emergency! You know who you are, so make sure your needs are taken care of!

CELL PHONE

If you have a CDMA phone (Verizon, Sprint, UScell, or Cricket), it's no good in EC for the most part. There is one exception, CNT, but it's very iffy so I would not treat it as an option. It's best if you purchase a GSM phone[46] in the US because phones are expensive

in EC. Don't forget to insure that it is unlocked and not under contract with a provider! *See more about unlocking your phone in the* **Before You Leave** *section.*

Take your passport, your unlocked GSM phone, and about 5,000 colones ($10 USD) to either Movistar, Claro, or CNT. Purchase a new prepaid sim card, or *prepago,* and put the rest of the money on the account so you have some minutes available for use. I would ask some folks in your neighborhood who they use. Do a little research to see which provider serves your area the best before you commit to a company. It's not as easy to keep your number in Ecuador as it is in North America. If you change companies, you can't port your number on prepaid sims.

Once you have determined the best provider, drop the sim card into your phone and find a really nice Ecuadorian to let you use their ID to set up the account, or if you have your cedula already, use the number

---

46 GSM phones in laymen's terms are the phones that use sim cards

off of your cedula when prompted! It can be a confusing set up process because all of the instructions are in Spanish. Try to have the provider, a friend, or a service assist you with the process.

If your town doesn't have internet providers, or you wish to have internet on the go with your laptop or other electronic device, you can purchase a 3G stick with one of the previously mentioned cellular providers.

INTERNATIONAL COMMUNICATION

Hopefully you've already set up your Skype account (or other provider mentioned), subscribed to the best unlimited calling plan for your situation, and purchased a unique phone number where business connections and loved ones can reach you. If not, read *Communication Set Up* in the *Before You Arrive section*.

If you have a smart phone, launch Skype and make a test call in the app. Make sure to dial from the Skype app, otherwise you will use airtime and long distance fees will apply!

Confirm that everyone you want to contact has a Skype account and knows how to log in. For the technologically challenged, I highly recommend you assist them in setting up their Skype so you can test out the connection.

To add someone to your Skype contacts, click "Contacts" at the top of your screen, then "Add Contact," then key in either their Skype username if you have it, or the email that they used to set up the account. This procedure needs to occur on both sides before you can be seen online and available for chatting on Skype.

Download and install TextPlus on your smart phone as mentioned in the *Before You Arrive* section. Send a trial text message to a loved one and have them send one back. You are up and running!

Don't forget about FaceTime for those who have Apple products. You can either connect by using their cell phone number or their Apple ID email address. Each route is free utilizing wifi for the connection.

TRANSPORTATION

PURCHASING A CAR

Buying a car in Ecuador is a bit different from purchasing one in North America. For starters, whatever car you're seeking will cost you many times more than it would in North America. A twenty-two year old Isuzu Rodeo with 200,000 Km (124,274 miles), manual transmission with a V6 engine, at the time of writing was advertised on *Patio de Autos* for $6,900! An equivalent car (Kelly Blue Book would only

date back to 1994 instead of 1992) is worth $754 in the United States!

Shopping for your vehicle can be done on a few different platforms. There isn't a Craigslist platform here, instead check:

- Mercado Libre[47]
- Patio Tuerca[48]
- Patio de Autos[49]

Since gas is just $1.48 per gallon, an old guzzler isn't as expensive on the road (after you own it outright that is).

While the cars are seemingly ancient, you would be surprised to see how well they are maintained. Many ten plus year old cars are spotless and rust-free! I guess I would keep a thick coat of wax on my car if I paid that much for it! The Sierras, in particular, have impeccably clean cars, probably because its dry and salt-free!

In fact, cars from the coast, or Guayas plates, have the stigma that they are inferior

---

[47] http://vehiculos.mercadolibre.com.ec

[48] http://ecuador.patiotuerca.com/

[49] http://www.patiodeautos.com

because they come from the land of salt and sand. If the license plate starts with a "G" then the car is from Guayas! The stigma is so strong that an equivalent car with the license plate beginning with an "A" (for Azuay) are more expensive!

If you're going to drop a ton of cash on some wheels, make sure and have a look under the hood! Take your car to a local mechanic to perform a cylinder compression test, it will only cost $5-10 and will tell you volumes about the car!

Once you find the right car, documents will need to be notarized (to the tune of $45), a wire transfer or certified check will buy the car (few more bucks) and if the car is currently registered, you will be all set until its due for renewal!

> **EXPAT EXPERIENCE**
>
> *"I bought my car second hand from a gringo client. He returned to the states immediately after purchasing a condo and a car in order to get his visa paperwork. After six months, he asked me to sell everything. I bought his car, a stick shift, not knowing how to drive a stick shift. The hard part was he wasn't physically here. You are both supposed to be present and get finger printed in order to notarize the sell. We had to do a lot of extra work to get the title transferred."*
> ~ Amy Prisco
> alprisco@gmail.com

ECUADORIAN DRIVER'S LICENSE

You are permitted to drive with your license from North America for one year after you arrive. After that initial year, you will need an Ecuador driver's license. There are many conflicting reports about how exactly to go about getting one. You'll read about taking a one week driving course, taking a written exam in Spanish, and so on. While the rules are constantly changing, here they are as of the writing of this book (reference becominganexpat.com for an updates between editions):

* Get an apostilled letter from the transit authority in your home country
* Have said letter translated into Spanish and notarized in Ecuador
* Take your cedula and driver's license along with copies of both to the nearest Agencia Nacional de Tránsito del Ecuador[50] (ANT, *Ecuador's equivalent to the DMV*)
* If you are not applying in Quito, then the office staff will scan your documents and send them to Quito for approval. Your approval should arrive within a couple of weeks
* Return to the ANT and see if your approval has arrived
* After you have your approval, you will be sent to the nearest eye and motor skills exam
* Take the eye and motor skills exam paperwork back to the ANT where you will take your written exam (Make certain they are giving exams

on the day you arrive. Oftentimes the office only tests two days a week.) They now offer exams in English in Salinas, Cuenca, and Quito. Once you pass the exam they will hand over a license!

TIP

The written exam is only 20 questions long, you can only miss 4 and still pass! Since the questions are drawn from a bank of 400 possibilities, some preparation is advised. On the ATN site you can download a PDF study exam and take online quizzes.

TAXIS

In large towns, taxis are plentiful and affordable running you just a dollar to most places in town. Long distance trips, on the other hand, can add up. Depending on the time of day, and how much business the driver has received throughout the day, a two hour drive may run you $100 bucks! A shuttle or renting a car for the day is

---

[50] http://bit.ly/ANTec

usually a better bet for long distance trips.

BUS

Learn the bus schedule applicable to your area. The link below contains the schedule throughout the country. If you wish to carry a printed schedule, you can pick one up at any bus station and most tourist centers. Buses are very inexpensive, averaging $1 per hour of drive time. Make sure you have change for the driver on local buses. For longer trips, purchase your ticket in the bollería at the bus terminal. Long distance buses are often sold with seating assignments so pay attention to the ticket. If it says *asiento* followed by a number, that is your seat assignment.

Make sure to arrive to the parrada (bus stop) fifteen minutes early because buses are occasionally ahead of schedule in EC.

www.ecuadorschedules.com

GATHER YOUR BEARINGS

The most frustrating part about moving for me was I had no idea where to get anything. For example, I needed an extension chord, an aux cable, and an adapter to go from the old stereo in my condo to an aux cable input. I hadn't the faintest clue where to find any of these items. I also had no idea how to say "Aux cable" in Spanish. My best shot was "hay un cable que usa para eschucar música en el carro?" Which is a really poor gringo way to say, "is there a cable that you use for listening to music in the car?" See what I mean? Stuff that usually requires zero brain power suddenly gobbles up endless energy!

In San Diego, I would simply Google Map the nearest Target and be on my way. Not so much in Ecuador, there aren't Home Depots. Even if there was an obvious retail outlet for my wanted item, there isn't an online venue to search the location of the nearest store. Many stores don't register with

Google, so they don't show up in a search. This is why your landlord, expat community, and tico friends are very valuable. They have already hunted down many of the items that you will need and want. If they haven't looked for it themselves, their buddy has and found it. Your network is gold! They will help answer:

- ☑ Where is the grocery store?
- ☑ Where is the gas station?
- ☑ Where is a good mechanic? (referral)
- ☑ Where can you buy hardware items?
- ☑ Where can you buy furniture?
- ☑ How do I find a handyman?
- ☑ Where do I pay my water bill?
- ☑ Where can I recharge my cell phone?
- ☑ When in doubt, roll with the flow, wait and then wait some more.

FILING FOR RESIDENCY

If your situation falls nicely within one of the visas listed in the *Immigration* section then as long as you dot your i's and cross your t's, the immigration process is fairly straightforward. That being said, navigating through the documents and deciphering which ones need to be apostilled and which ones need to be notarized and translated can be exhausting. There are numerous services that for a small fee will assist you throughout the entire immigration process. If you came equipped with your paperwork upon arrival to Ecuador, you could have your cedula (residency ID) within the first 30 days!

There are a variety of services that can assist you with the process. After concluding my research and interviews, the top two contenders would be:

- EcuaAssit[51] (offices in Cuenca, Manta, and Bahía de Caráquez)
- Visa specialist Dana Cameron (uses Guayaquil Immigration offices)

EXPAT EXPERIENCE

"Marcos and his staff were fantastic. I cannot recommend them highly enough. He took great care of us and we wouldn't change a think if we had to do it over again."
~ Bev & James Petersen expats from Wisconsin

See more expat experiences in the **Resources & Services** section.

EXPAT EXPERIENCE

"In order to get our visa, cedula, and censor, we used a total of three different people: Maite, Catalina, and Dana. Dana was our favorite. Dana would meet us in Guayaquil each time we had the paperwork to submit. She knew most of the people there because she taught them in college. I had a couple of papers that were Appostled there and it never cost me more money. Our visa cost exactly what she said it would.

After the 10 plus trips to Cuenca for our visas with Maite and Catalina, Dana was a breath of fresh air."
~ Diane Bublack, expat from West Virgina

ESTATE PLANNING

Having your affairs in order is important no matter where you live. When you add the extra complication of an international residency, you need to take extra care in your arrangements for the unfortunate possibility of personal or spousal demise. Death is scary, horrible, and unavoidable... So we need to plan for it. We don't want to leave our grieving loved ones in a bind. That's the last thing anyone wants.

EXPAT EXPERIENCE

"In December, shortly after we bought our condo, my love became ill... On Christmas eve I took him to the hospital, he never saw his lovely condo again. After many tests we were told he had leukemia and had to go back to the US because they only had two units of his rare AB Negative blood type. My platelets were compatible so we did that and headed back to the US on the 27th of Dec. I lost him to the awful blood cancer on the 14th of January 2012 just two days before his 67th birthday."
~ Connie Wilson, expat since 2011

Consult an attorney from your home country to see how to organize your will to assure that your international residency won't complicate matters. If you purchase property, cars, or maintain an Ecuadorian bank account after arriving into EC you should take your US will to an Ecuadorian estate planner and create an Ecuadorian will.

Your US will can function in Ecuador as long as it doesn't contradict Ecuadorian law. In Ecuadorian law your children are the first heirs to the estate, after which follows parents, and if there aren't living children or parents then it falls on living siblings. If your will does not agree with this order it will be null and void managing Ecuadorian assets. Your loved ones in Ecuador will have to pay an inheritance tax if the assets handed down total more than $64,000 USD.

Take care to include your burial or cremation wishes in the document. This decision is extremely personal, and in some circumstances religious. I will warn you, repatriating a body to your home country will cost you a fortune (if it's not covered with your insurance). Plus, it can be a bit logistically challenging if the body is leaving the hot and humid coastal region. If at all possible, opt to be buried in EC or cremated.

_____

Further Reading: Informative article explaining Estate Planning laws in Ecuador provided by EcuaAssist[52]

---

[52] http://bit.ly/ECwill

PART III CHECK LIST

☐ Make a budget to kill your debts.

☐ Assess your current bank and credit cards for international compatibility. Make changes as applicable.

☐ Obtain or renew passport(s).

☐ Renew drivers license if applicable.

☐ Gather immigration documents (see immigration section).

☐ Decide what to do with your stuff.

☐ If shipping a container, request at least three estimates from reputable movers.

☐ Decide which electronics you want to take with you and purchase the electronics that you need for the move.

☐ If you are a smart phone or tablet kinda' gal/guy, download and play with the best apps for expats.

☐ Make sure you have an unlocked GSM phone.

☐ Create a Skype account and share it with loved ones and business colleagues.

☐ Download a free text messaging app and try it out. Give your contacts your new texting number before you leave.

☐ Prep your car for sale, advertise and sell *(Carmax is a great option I have used twice)*.

PART IV
FAMILY & EDUCATION

Moving abroad with kids. Does it hinder or harm their future? Raising kids in Ecuador

MOVING WITH A FAMILY

Uprooting your family in the pursuit of something better is a scary prospect. North Americans have been conditioned from a very young age that their homeland is the best and most sought after country in the world. The truth is, the best is not the same from one family to another. One country does not fit all, and Ecuador is no exception.

I'm compelled to remind you there is nothing new about seeking social and economic opportunities elsewhere. Humans are migratory beings. Long before the westward movement, people migrated to richer pastures in order to increase their quality of life and, in some cases, to survive. I am a strong proponent of thriving not surviving.

With big business encroaching on middle America, education at a record low, healthcare costs seeming endless, poverty and unemployment at record highs, and quality of life on the decline, many people have decided now is the time to look elsewhere.

EXPAT EXPERIENCE

"In Ecuador, the fathers take a very active parenting role. They carry the babies, watch over the young children, teach them to swim, and play with the older kids. I observed a bus driver with his wife and daughter. The daughter asked her father to hold her baby. So he took her baby doll, tucked it up under his shoulder strap on the seat belt and continued his drive. Even after the daughter fell asleep, he left her baby doll right there. He didn't seem at all bothered that every passenger coming and going saw him holding his child's baby doll. It is very impressive to see such interaction between fathers and kids."
~ Connie Wilson, expat from Houston

Below are a few important questions commonly asked by parents considering migration:

Would I be helping or hindering my children's growth and opportunities? Would we be able to return if we decided it was best for the kids? Is it safe? What is the cost of school?

Moving your family from your place of residence is an extremely personal decision. My goal is to fully inform and answer any questions you have so you can make the best decision for your family. Remember, no decision is a decision in itself. Now, let's address these common concerns.

EDUCATION IN EC

I'll give you the bad news first. Some studies place Ecuador with the lowest quality of education in Latin America! All children are required by law to attend school until they achieve a "basic level of education" which is often considered just nine years. Only 71% of kids stay enrolled through fifth grade!

The government ended tuition fees many years ago for the public universities, making them free for those who could gain admittance through aptitude tests. Even with free education, only 15% of students enrolled graduate.

Ecuador's literacy rate, 92%, places them 122nd out of 194 countries.

The public schools in Ecuador are often consider ill-equipped. The quality of education ranges greatly from school to school. Content-wise, expats have reported their newly enrolled kids are behind in some subjects and ahead in others.

The most important criteria for many expat parents is accreditation. They want their children to have as many options and open doors as possible.

There are three different degrees that a child can earn while attending school in Ecuador:

☐ The Ecuadorian Bachillerato Diploma makes your child eligible to apply for college in Ecuador.

☐ The International Baccalaureate (IB) Diploma, accredited by the International Baccalaureate Organization in Geneva Switzerland is the most flexible option. This degree makes you eligible to apply for college in the USA, Europe, and Latin America.

☐ The USA High School Diploma is available at every American private school and online through the many homeschool programs (i.e. K-12). This diploma enables you to apply to colleges in the USA, Europe, and many other countries.

Currently, there are seventy-four schools[53] that offer the IB diploma in Ecuador! *Sebastián de Benalcázar* in Quito is one of twenty public high schools that are attempting the transition into the IB Diploma.

Expats have the same three options for schooling that their peers have in their hometown:

[53] http://bit.ly/ECIBschools

homeschool, private school, and public school.

Oftentimes, foreigners choose to place their children in private English taught schools so their child acclimates more smoothly, without a language barrier. Others opt for full immersion through Spanish speaking schools so their children will become bi-lingual more quickly. The latter option is harder for the first six months to a year but after the hump, their kids are bi-lingual and thereby can acclimate easier with their newly acquired language skills.

Now for the *good* news! There are a variety of ways to homeschool and obtain a US or IB diploma for little to no money! Also, there are hundreds of private English-taught schools across Ecuador.

HOMESCHOOLING

Homeschooling has gained popularity both in the States and abroad. The only difference is really where "home" is. Homeschooling in Ecuador can be challenging when considering activities designed for groups of participants of the same age.

K-12.com

This site allows you to navigate through international education options from a variety of schools ranging from public to preparatory. If you maintain an address in the US and pay taxes in that state *(maybe a family member's address for your mail)*, you can select the corresponding state and enroll in online public school.

Many states require you to start the program while in-state, so make sure to set up your education options before you leave the area. In-person "Start-Up Success" sessions are often provided to introduce the student to the online learning setting. While you're there, they also develop customized Individualized Learning Plans (ILP). If your program requires textbooks, make sure and get as many as you can prior to leaving. Purchasing books and shipping them to EC can be a bit of a hassle (see *Mail* in the *Before You Leave* section).

Most K-12 programs offer college level courses so that your student can begin to earn college credits while in high school!

Go to www.k-12.com to learn more.

TIP

A common conversation starter with Ecuadorian kids is asking what grade they are in. Their answers may leave you confused due to the old way they count grades.

Kindergarten   =   Jardin
1st to 6th grade   =   1st to 6th grado (grade)
7th to 12th grade =   1st to 6th curso (course)

While they no longer refer to grades this way officially, it takes awhile to break the habit, so you will still hear grades referred to this way.

The official way to count grades is by years in school.

Kindergarten   =   1st año (year)
12th grade   =   13th año (year)

PRIVATE SCHOOLS

There are hundreds of private school options and just as many price-tags. Most private schools that teach in English are located in Quito, Guayaquil, and Cuenca.

Private schools offer a variety of diploma options, some like the *Colegio Americano de Quito,* offer all three!

Below are a few private schools that are vouched for by expat parents.

Quito

Colegio Menor San Francisco de Quito
http://colegiomenor.edu.ec
- classes taught in English
- college counselors onsite who help you secure scholarships
- extensive sport and art programs

Colegio Americano de Quito
www.fcaq.k12.ec

- Choose from any degree options for your child's diploma
- Non-profit, secular school founded by a former president of Ecuador

Acadamia Cotopaxi
www.cotopaxi.k12.ec
- Acadamia Cotopaxi was the first school in Ecuador to receive authorization to offer the IB Diploma program

Alliance Academy International
www.alliance.k12.ec

SEK - Quito International School
(located in San Isidro de El Inca)
www.sekquito.com
email: sekquito@sekquito.com

SEK - Los Valles International School (located in Cumbaya, Quito)
www.seklosvalles.ec
Email:
seklosvalles@seklosvalles.com

Colegio Experimental Britanico Internacional
www.colegiobritanico.edu.ec

Guayaquil

InterAmerican Academy
www.interamerican.edu.ec
Email:
info@interamerican.edu.ec
- private and nonprofit
- US degree
- 2 Semesters (Early August - mid-December then early July to late May)
- Grades 1-5 = $10,920 USD p/yr
- Grades 9-12 = $12,730 USD p/yr

A great resource in your hunt for private schools is www.portaldelcolegio.com. Simply click on schools and colleges under "select your search" and you can weed through hundreds of schools looking for those that meet your monetary criteria.

PUBLIC SCHOOLS

Would I be helping or hindering my children's growth and opportunities?

Don't take my word for it. Schedule an appointment with potential colleges and employers in respectable fields. Ask them how they would respond to a potential student or employee with international experience. What I believe you will discover is that an international upbringing adds quality, diversity, and growth that no other program or school could match.

At the very least, your child will be bi-lingual, have successfully acclimated into another culture and way of life (huge points in both college entry and employment), and have learned life skills and experienced self-growth unmatched by a peer that remained in the United States. I would have loved an international upbringing.

Outside of resumés and college entry brownie points, your child will learn about nature through experiencing it with all five senses! There is no museum required in order to experience biology in Ecuador. Gone are the days the football team acquired the monies previously allocated for the arts.

Home life could refocus around the family. The work culture is very lax. An affordable family centric life is the norm and the expected way of life in Ecuador. Since life is less expensive, you would be able to take breaks from your work to play with, talk to, and shape your own children's lives! Gone are the days of depending on daycare or school to raise YOUR children, a dream come true for many!

Your path would not be without bumps. The transition time may be very difficult on you and your kids. If your kids are adolescents, it can be particularly rough. Language acquisition will be harder and their self-consciousness will hinder their language expression. Teenagers undoubtedly experience hardship finding their place in the world. They want to be different and the same all at once. If you add a new culture and language into an already volatile time, you can expect an explosion.

That being said, every child is unique and how they handle change can be dramatically different from child to child. Moving to Ecuador could be the best thing you could do for your teenager. Only you know what's best for your kids. Don't let society or me tell you what your kids need.

Would we be able to return if we decided that it was best for the kids?

The answer to this question is very much dependent on your planning. If you are not fully committed to the idea of moving your family to Ecuador, why not commit to a year? Save up enough emergency cash to fly everyone home and pay for at least three months of bills.

If you own your home and have gained a handsome amount of equity, you have a choice to make. You can either cash out, have your safety pile of cash, and rent in Ecuador, or you can hire a rental agency to rent your US home and rent in Ecuador.

The risk is not equal for each option. If you choose the cash out option and Ecuador doesn't work out, then you could possibly have a difficult time finding a comparable house or the same interest rate you locked into years ago.

The market, however, is unpredictable. Take the market in 2002, for example. If you had sold and moved to Ecuador from California just before the crash, you would have likely doubled your money! Decide what's most important to you, the money upfront or the security of owning a home with potential rental income.

As far as schooling goes, if you were homeschooling, your kids won't miss a beat. If your kids were in an Ecuadorian school, there may be a bit of re-acclimation but no unsurpassable hurdles there.

Work

As far as work is concerned, why not take your work with you? You would be surprised how many jobs are telecommuting friendly.[54] If your employer or your industry is not, start looking for something else that is, or start something

---

[54] See the Telecommuting section for more information

new! EC is an exciting country to start a new business in.[55]

If you packed your work and took it with you then you would not be at risk of losing your income by moving abroad or globe trotting for that matter. In fact, the move would have increased your marketability. You could add: bi-lingual, an international specialist, or an international consultant on your brag list.

Is it safe?

Safety is on every parent's mind. I don't mean to be too philosophical but what is safety? Do rules make it safe? Do low criminal statistics make it safe? Safety to me is a feeling, a vibe. I feel very safe in Ecuador, and if I had children, I would certainly bring them here.

While your child would have to be more careful in school to avoid having their belongings stolen, they wouldn't have to worry about bullies, teen suicides, and mass murders like in the United States.

Personally, I'd rather deal with petty theft over school shootings.

While Ecuador has NEVER had a mass murder, a terrorist attack, or a school shooting, they do have armed robberies. Muggers don't target kids, of course, but it's something to consider.

Statistically, Ecuador has higher crime in Quito and Guayaquil. Petty theft is the most common crime so if you leave valuables in your car, consider it a donation.

I don't believe the statistics accurately represent the population because many Ecuadorians do not report incidents, instead they take matters into their own hands.

In Ecuador, children are free to roam the streets and play with the neighborhood kids without fear. While the cities are not crime free, the culture is not fear-driven as in the States. Ecuadorians live life more freely. What a gift that could be to your child.

---

[55] See more about starting a business in Ecuador in the Work Hard Play Hard section

What is the cost of school?

Public schools are free and are taught in Spanish. They rarely have international accreditation.

Private schools range from $300 per month to $1300 per month and are taught in numerous languages with varying accreditations.

ACCLIMATING THE CHILDREN

ADJUSTING TO A NEW SCHOOL, LANGUAGE, ACTIVITIES, AND EXPLORATION

If at all possible, plan your move so the kids have time to acclimate before school starts. Hire a private Spanish tutor for them and you while you're still living in the States. Make learning Spanish a family endeavor. Play Spanish Jeopardy, Apples to Apples (Spanish version), or other language acquisition games together for game night

After arriving in Ecuador, sign up for intensive Spanish classes as a family for at least two weeks, preferably a month. You might not all be in the same class because your language levels may vary, but you will all be able to practice your Spanish together which will greatly assist your adjustment. If you or your spouse is struggling with the move, it will certainly reflect on your children's experience. So set yourself up for success.

ACTIVITIES

Make sure that moving to Ecuador is an adventure for the kids. You may have visited Ecuador in the past and the kids enjoyed it as a vacation. This expectation is hard to come back from when transiting vacation life to real life. Make sure and plan fun activities.

Let them be part of the planning process. Give them assignments like "Explore the back yard and see if there would be a good spot for compost or a small garden." If they're old enough, have them research how to compost and build a compost bin / drum /stack for use in your yard. Find ways to connect their hobbies with the natural assets Ecuador has to offer. My teenage brother-in-law built a zip-line and platform 50 feet up a tree with his dad! Other activities could include:

☐ Creating a scavenger hunt consisting of flora and fauna, birds, and frogs known to be in the area for them to take a picture of and identify. Then compare notes and see how many points they got! Reward the points with a trip to the beach, park, pool, or nearby waterfall!

☐ Bring a picnic to a nearby waterfall and enjoy the serenity.

☐ Feed the iguanas.

☐ Go on "adventure walks" together with a wildlife guidebook, learning and identifying new plants, insects, and animals each day.

☐ Take Spanish lessons from the same school and have homework sessions together.

☐ Once a month, let a child pick somewhere new to explore within a given range. If you can afford a weekend away once a month or once every two months, this would be a great way to get to know the country.

☐ Google "solar carving" and learn this fantastic way to use the sun's energy as your paint brush by engraving the wood through burning! A much better use of the magnifying glass than killing ants! Pick up a cheap pair of welding glasses from a hardware store.

☐ Buy cheap digital cameras (possibly disposable) and have photo contests! The winner gets to choose what's for dinner from a list of possibilities!

☐ Put a blanket down on the ground outside after dark and star gaze. Use an iPhone app, Skywalker, to help you identify the constellations. You can either tell the corresponding Greek mythology stories or make up new ones. You start the story then tag the person to your right to continue the story, and so on.

Key points to keep in mind are: language acquisition, change of schedule and expectations, making new friends, and getting them connected in the community so they have a sense of purpose. For teenagers, it is of utmost importance that they make it on their own. Support any healthy hobbies or interests they express. Make sure they have the freedom to find things that interest them.

When you run out of ideas, Pinterest is an excellent resource. Just search for things to do outside, craft ideas, gardening, things to do for free, and so on!

PART V

WORK & BUSINESS

A GUIDE TO STARTING A BUSINESS IN ECUADOR OR OPERATING ONE
INTERNATIONALLY

WORK HARD PLAY HARD

Not Retired?

You are never too young to move to EC. It's a land for the wise, the adventurers, and the peace seekers. Herds of 20 and 30 somethings dissatisfied with the rat race are looking for alternative lifestyles elsewhere. Other closer destinations, such as Costa Rica, are no longer as affordable. Ecuador is becoming a frontier land.

STARTUPS IN ECUADOR

Without the hurdles of large industry that encompass entrepreneurship in the US, EC is exceedingly hospitable to small businesses. Start up fees are modest, making it a great place to try out a product or service without taking extraordinary risks.

Whether you own a business in the US, EC, or South Africa, you must satisfy a need in order to be successful.

Examine your market and see where gaps exist. If you hope to serve the community you live in, find out what needs are not being met. If you hope to serve an international community online, find a niche that you are passionate about and can easily satisfy from any location in the world.

Once you decide what type of business you want to create, set out with a business and marketing plan. You will need to decide in which country to register the business, Ecuador or your home country.

One side of my business, Enete Enterprises, entails filming and producing two minute marketing videos for adventure tours, destinations, hotels, real estate, and special events. In Ecuador, I can stroll into a hotel or tour agency with my iPad and easily obtain an audience with the decision maker and share what I can do for them.

In the US, it takes months of redirection, red tape, and dismissals before I may or may not gain an audience with the decision maker. Enete Enterprises, LLC is a US based company that conducts business in a variety of countries.

There is a huge market for tourism, niche group travel, retirement, medical tourism, eco-living, alternative living, health, and self-sustaining properties just to name a few. If you were to open a hotel or tour business in Ecuador, you would need to register it with the Ecuadorian authorities.

According to the World Bank Doing Business report for

2014,[56] Ecuador ranks 135/185 for ease of doing business (dropping one slot since 2013). The same report also states, on average, it takes 55.5 days to open the doors as a new business in Ecuador. The longest wait was for your inspection and operations permit from the municipality (29 days).

On the plus side, they rank 86/185 in regard to securing credit.

EXPAT QUOTE

"When you're in business here, you have people who rely on you and depend on you. So every word you say is golden and has to be true. The sense of time, responsibility, and consequence doesn't exist amongst most locals. This is why working as the intermediary between the government and gringos can be challenging. It's ultimately rewarding, but challenging."

~ Amy Prisco, owner of REMAX Salinas
alprisco@gmail.com

CREATING A BUSINESS IN ECUADOR 101

Take time to consider the best way to incorporate and the location in which to file your business when you enter the world of entrepreneurship. Ask your experienced accountant about incorporating prior to doing so. Incorporation requires a great deal of paperwork and expense and provides little to no benefits. Once incorporated, you are held accountable to countless ever changing laws and in order to dissolve the corporation, you will spend months completing the paperwork and nursing the resulting paper cuts. The take home message is really do your homework prior to taking action.

---

[56] For the full report: http://www.doingbusiness.org/data/exploreeconomies/ecuador

Consider your market. Are they Ecuadorian people or businesses, are they North Americans, or is your service or product without borders?

If after seeking counsel from experienced business owners, and speaking with an Ecuadorian attorney you have decided to start a business in Ecuador, the following list will guide your path over the next two months.

☐ Reserve the company name with the Superintendent of Companies (online procedure).[57]

☐ Hire a lawyer to prepare the minutes of incorporation $500-900. (Minutes will include the Constituting contract, Articles of Incorporation, Bylaws, and the formation of capital) Your lawyer will sign the documents and have a third party notarize them.

☐ Deposit 50% of the capital into a bank account set up under the name of the company, or *integración de capital.*

☐ Have your lawyer present the documents above (with three certified copies of the charter and the Bylaws) to the Superintendent of Companies for the approval of the company's incorporate.

☐ Publish an abstract of the charter in a daily newspaper that circulates where the company operates.

☐ Inscribe the company's charter and resolutions, as

well as the name of the company's legal representatives, in the Mercantile Registry Office.

☐ Apply for the Registro Unico de Contribuyentes (RUC).

☐ Print invoices and VAT forms at an authorized printing shop.

☐ Sign up online for Social Security- Instituto Ecuatoriano de Seguridad Social (IESS) and obtain a password to get approval of payroll forms and be issued an Employer's identification number. Employees must sign a contract that is then registered with the Ministry of Labor.

☐ Share all employee contracts with the Ministry of Labor (Inspectoria de Trabajo)

☐ Receive inspection and operations permit from the municipality.

☐ Obtain *"tasa de habilitación"* and pay commercial patent at the municipality.

To form a Corporation in Ecuador, you must have a minimum capitol pay in of $800. Don't worry about being a foreign owner, the law clearly permits the owner(s) to be foreigner(s). The average cost to start a business in Ecuador runs between $1500 - $2000 USD.

After you have your business up and running, be prepared to publish your financial statements in a local paper twice a year!

TIP

"I have a RUC because we are in charge of our unregistered Home Owners Insurance. Anyway, an Ecuadorian official recently shared with me, "You realize since you have a RUC, if you put money (about 12%)in your SS account, you will qualify to get social security when you age out." Great news, social security from two countries! I'm looking forward to turning 65."
~ Diane Bublack, expat from West Virginia

DOING BUSINESS

Ecuador, like every country has its own unique work culture. In order to be successful, you need to learn about said culture and how to incorporate it into how you conduct business.

North Americans are often quick firing, wheel and deal type of business people. If you are quick and to the point in the US, the time saved is greatly appreciated since time is the highest valued commodity. That business culture doesn't translate or get the job done in Ecuador. Instead, regular social gatherings, sharing meals, and talking about your family is what gets the job done here.

Ecuadorians need to trust you in order to do business with you. They don't trust what they don't know. Expect to be drilled over every aspect of your private and public life before an Ecuadorian commits to working a deal with you.

> **TIP**
>
> Spending time to get to know Ecuadorians doesn't just apply to business, it applies to everything. Take buying a house, for instance. If you take the owners out for a few beers and chit chat with them, you may find yourself purchasing the house for your desired price.

Ecuadorians arriving to meetings one to two hours late is the norm. So much so, they don't even find it necessary to offer an apology for their tardiness. Learning to account for this rule will save you many headaches.

Ecuador is very much a "man's world." Women are just beginning to enter the work force and are very rarely offered a position with power. Many Ecuadorians find it difficult or unpleasant to take orders or make business deals with a woman.

Another thing to ask yourself is what type of work culture do you fit in? Do you like a relaxed, informal laissez-faire attitude about your business? Or do you wear pleats, iron your shirts and enjoy a serious work environment?

Work atmospheres vary drastically from the coast to the Sierras. If you want a chilled back work vibe, your business will fit right in with the cool nonchalant vibes offered up by the coastal locals. If you prefer your business to be taken more seriously, less laughing more typing type of situation, then head to Quito.

> **TIP**
>
> Don't hold breakfast meetings. By stereotype, Ecuadorians are not morning folks. Also, if you are offered coffee at a meeting, don't ask if they have tea. Ecuadorians are incredibly proud of their coffee, so pretend to enjoy it.

HIRING / FIRING ECUADORIANS

Before you decide to hire Ecuadorians for your business, or to clean your house, study Ecuadorian labor laws carefully. They are drastically different from the laws in the US with heavy support for the worker.

When you have decided to employ a worker full-time, you must offer them a worker contract that serves to protect both parties and clarify expectations. It is extremely important that you create a well-worded, clear employment contract.

All contracts begin with a three month trial term where either party can terminate the arrangement. The minimum employment term after the preliminary three months is one year and the maximum is two years. After those two years, you and your employee can enter an indefinite term.

Pay close attention here... this first three months is the ONLY time an employer can terminate an employee without strict process and potential remuneration for their years of service.

In order to fire an employee the employer, must obtain authorization from the Ministry of Labor and Human Resources. It's like a game of *Mother May I* but with much more paperwork.

The burden of proof is on the employer to demonstrate why the employee must be let go. Because of this, take care to keep diligent records with specific acts, dates, and times if you think the termination of an employee is warranted. If the Ministry of Labor disagrees with you and does not grant your approval, the employee is automatically entitled to three months remuneration payable for service lasting up to three years as a minimum. If they worked for you for three or more years, one month's remuneration for each year, up to twenty-five months salary is due. A fraction of a year is considered a complete year for purposes of payment.

Traditionally, Ecuadorians are paid for nine public holidays and are given an additional fifteen days of paid leave. Each year of service earns them an additional day per year of vacation time.

Many folks decide that for their small business it makes more sense to avoid all of the complications of hiring full-time staff by hiring independent contractors (IC). So instead of hiring two full-time workers, they might hire 4 ICs.

SOCIAL SECURITY

As you read above, you must register your company with the Social Security Administration. One of the administration's jobs is to assure that your employees are not being exploited. They can serve in a similar way as unions have served the States.

Expat Quote
"Mañana doesn't mean tomorrow, it means not today." ~ Amy Prisco

LATIN TIME

Plan for the fact that you will be working in a country that honors the siesta. Part of Ecuador's draw is its slow pace and relaxed atmosphere. That fact will clearly present itself in your business experience, so plan for it.

It is all too easy to revert back to your North American workaholic business habits with healthy doses of stress and urgency. Don't fall back into these habits. Plan to work within the tempo of the nation, and the tempo established in your business plan.

If you're business is effected by the ebb and flow of tourists from season to season, plan ahead for the low season. If your business is related to the tourism sector in any way, you will experience great revenue swings month to month. Make sure you stock away a nest egg on those winning months, so you can make it through the economic droughts.

EXPORTING TO ECUADOR

In 2012, President Obama announced the National Export Initiave (NEI)[58] in an effort to increase US exports to Ecuador. The predictability of Ecuador's trade policy has been difficult as of late. The government is experimenting with ways to improve trade due to the constant flux in its current petroleum-based economy. The last four years we have seen policies that are direct opposites of one another.

---

[58] http://www.export.gov

They certainly keep exporters on the edge of their seats![59]

If you don't want to start your own exporting business, you could work for an Ecuadorian company that exports to the US? Hundreds of native English speakers are hired in Ecuador's export sector because the nation's principal trading partner is the U.S. The Export and Investment Promotion Corporation of Ecuador[60] maintains a database of exporters which could be helpful in your job search. Also, Ecuador's chambers of commerce can also be of use locating exporters.

TELECOMMUTING

An increasing number of companies are seeing the win-win in telecommuting. They can lower overhead with utilities and real estate costs, and increase employee morale and productivity by allowing them to choose the environment they thrive in.

If your employer doesn't currently use telecommuters, don't worry, it doesn't mean they won't allow it. You must be savvy and take care how you present the offer. I recommend you read *The Work From Home Handbook*[61] by Diana Fitzpatrick and Stephen Fishman before you pitch to your boss. The book will help polish your pitch in order to speak their language and address their fears or concerns, before they even realized they had any.

If you don't have a job or your employer has closed the telecommuting door, then it may be time to look in another direction.

What are you experienced in? What can you bring to the table? Who would benefit from your skills? If you have worked in sales, how can you reshape yourself as an international asset?

---

[59] For more information about exporting to Ecuador read: http://ecuador.usembassy.gov/doing-business-local.html

[60] www.corpei.org

[61] http://bit.ly/workfromhomedf

How is it working out for you living in Puerto Cayo and traveling internationally regularly for work? *"I work from home and communicate through email, Skype, magic jack or any other electronic means. I develop training curriculum for two separate organizations. Traveling presents minor inconveniences. The trip from Puerto Cayo to Guayaquil is a two-hour drive. If I were to hire a driver, this would be roughly $75 a trip. During the first two years, due to the 90-day restriction* (you can't leave Ecuador for more than 90 days in your first two years of residency), *working has been a bit more challenging. I can only travel to train for those 90 days. My flights generally leave late at night. I pass through customs and get my passport stamped at about 2100, but my flight does not leave until 0130. The return trip is generally the same way, so I get charged an extra day on each end of the trip. The trips do afford me the opportunity to bring back stuff from the States. Due to my flight status, I am allowed extra luggage, so bringing home supplies for Mark and me and our friends is the norm.*

And I would like to add that the customs employees will indeed take your cedula if you bust the 90 days (experience talking here). This will ultimately cost you another two or three trips to Guayaquil to process the paperwork again."
~ Diane Bublack, expat and consultant from West Virginia

INDEPENDENT CONSULTANT

If you have worked during your lifetime then you have experience in something. Think about what you're good at and see if you can pull together a market you can help through consultations.

There are a variety of business opportunities in Ecuador with new business owners in every sector. These new owners need help with a variety of niches: marketing, social media, customer service practices, IT, website development, content creators, multi-media, international accounting, productivity, import/export, etc.

PROPERTY MANAGEMENT & REAL ESTATE

With more and more expats looking abroad to spend their "golden years" in a place that allows for a higher quality of life and young professionals looking for an international experience, real estate has opened up dramatically in Ecuador over the last few years.

With the wealthiest and largest group of people entering their retirement years, this market is expected to explode.

Ecuador does require a real estate license in order to work as an agent or broker. The course and exam is in Spanish, so excellent language skills would really help your process.

Don't expect to be signed as an exclusive buyer or seller agent. That's not how it works down here. Instead, it's a free for all. Your clients can hire as many agents as they desire, the winner sells the property and reaps all of the rewards.

In addition to sales, property management is also a promising market. That's not to say it's easy money. Anyone who has experience maintaining property in a foreign country will tell you that it's incredibly challenging and time consuming, especially if you don't have excellent handymen and a grasp of Spanish in your arsenal. Numerous Ecuadorians and expats alike have second homes in EC. These homes need to be watched, maintained, and rented out in order to produce supplement income. With the humidity along the coastal regions of Ecuador, a house left unkept can literally rot.

JOB SEARCH

You can begin your job search online before you arrive! Cruise the classified on Ecuador's online newspapers:
• El Comercio (Quito)
• El Hoy (Quito)
• El Universo (Guayaquil)
• El Mercurio (Cuenca)

Ads for English teaching jobs frequently appear in the weekend and Monday editions of the online and print newspapers. If you're looking to land a teaching job, you should also check out TEFL websites:
• Dave's ESL Café www.eslcafe.com
• TEFL.com
• ITTT: www.tesolcourse.com/ tesol-jobs/ecuador

TEACHING ENGLISH

You can easily earn your TESOL or TEFL certificate online or in the classroom, making you eligible to apply for teaching jobs around the world. Most employers require you to be a native English speaker, and have taken a 120 hour course in either TESOL or TEFL. Some also require a Bachelor's degree in any subject.

In Ecuador, most TESOL/ TEFL jobs I've seen advertised have been in and around the Quito and Guayaquil regions. There are hundreds of schools and universities that offer English classes, so there is no lacking of need for English teachers.

If you're hoping to live in a region that doesn't seem to have teaching opportunities through an agency, then consider tutoring privately. Talk to neighbors and find out who wants to hire an English teacher.

While taking your TEFL certification, it's possible to specialize in "young learner" or "business English" thereby adding marketability and greater appeal to land a job in your preferred target audience.

I received my TESOL certificate through International TEFL and TESOL Training. I chose the 120 unit course and completed it online with my spouse. They allowed us to turn in one homework per unit since we would be completing it together. Each assignment we turned in was reviewed by our tutor, Earl. If any changes needed to be made, Earl sent it back with remarks. I have no complaints and would recommend them:

http://bit.ly/TEFLTESOL

English teachers average $300-$500 monthly salary in Ecuador.

NGOs & FOUNDATIONS

There are numerous NGOs and foundations operating in Ecuador. Many of these operations are in need of English speaking staff in administration, fundraising, marketing, and other job classifications. Monthly salary can range from $350-$1000. Be advised, however, the government has taken a stern stance against NGOs over the last three years, closing numerous companies across the country.

TOURISM JOBS

Tourism is a multi-billion dollar industry. As mentioned before, the baby boomers are just beginning to enter into their retirement as the most wealthy group the world has ever seen. What do they all have in common? They all want to travel.

Group travel has always sported a healthy market and is seeing large increases in demand. This means you could hop on an established tour group as a tour director after you earn your certificate through the International Guide Academy: www.bepaidtotravel.com).

Or if you'd rather guide than direct, become a specialized guide for a niche group: LGBT, Food, Wine, Coffee, Grandparent, or Children tours to name a few. You can earn guide

certification through the National Tour Association: www.ntaonline.com. In addition to an international license, you will need to obtain your certification as a tour guide from the Ministry of Tourism in Ecuador. (You can earn $50-$100 a day plus tips.)

If you're a *behind the scenes* kind of person and have an artistic eye, you can secure work designing those flashy tourism brochures and website content.

WORK VISAS

Securing a work visa in Ecuador is much easier than in many other Latin American countries. However, it usually requires hiring an attorney. You will need to demonstrate that you are filling a position an Ecuadorian does not have the capabilities to fill (i.e. English language, healthcare, IT, Biotech, and International Business skills).

You will need a letter from the company that is offering you a position specifying why they are contracting you and what importance you will have to their company. You must obtain a RUC number. Usually your employer assists you with this process, however, it must be completed in the Ecuadorian consulate in your country of origin.

TIP

Once you arrive in Ecuador, start your job search with notice boards at coffee shops, internet cafes, and hostels. If you're in Quito, La Mariscal, the city's main tourist district, often has extensive notice boards. The South American Explorers Club (on Jorge Washington, a few blocks east of Avenida 6 de Diciembre), posts job listings. These postings are usually for bar-tending, hospitality, teaching, and volunteer positions. You'll see more work opportunities from May through September (the high season).

JOBS "OFF THE BOOKS"

Under the table jobs are more often sought out by younger folks without kids.

This book does not endorse working illegally, it simply acknowledges that it occurs.

Undocumented jobs often include: restaurant work, bi-lingual tourism jobs (often owned by expats), flier distributer, sales, marketing, etc.

Do not expect to get paid much by working under the table. The minimum wage for legal workers in Ecuador is $340 per month which is $22 more than last year's minimum wage. That works out to just $2.20 an hour.

VIRTUAL OFFICE 101

Telecommuting, independent contracting, creative arts, and the freedoms provided by the worldwide web, make working from any location around the world limited only by your creativity and bandwidth.[62]

In order to work from your dream location, you will need to establish a framework. This can include but is not limited to setting up an email account,

---

[62] Internet signal strength

online banking, international communication solutions, business numbers in each country code necessary, mail forwarding services, securing a US address, purchasing a laptop and any devices required for connectivity to the internet.[63]

After the basics are set up, you will need to create an environment conducive to work and productivity. A space free from distractions, one that you can also walk away from when it's quitting time. Consider what you want your work hours to be? Are you more creative and productive in the morning or late at night?

Many 8 to 5'ers are not accustomed to the variety and freedoms allotted to those who work from home. Find out what works best for you. Experiment with your schedule until you find the best flow.

Most people feel their best with a regular sleep and rise schedule, a morning shower, eat breakfast, and get dressed for the day before they attempt to contribute to society. This is still true if you work from home. Just because you can work in your PJs doesn't necessarily mean you should.

Do not neglect your self-care each day. Take time to exercise, eat, and take breaks. It's absolutely imperative that you have a start and stop time! Telecommuting doesn't mandate that you work 24 hours a day. Just because your office and laptop are one room away, doesn't mean you are on call 24/7. You need to set clear boundaries for yourself and those you work with. Creating a balanced schedule and sticking to it is key for a successful balance of life, family, and business.

A friend of mine, Corey Coates, owns a Podcast production company (Podfly) in addition to working for a second company as a program director. He shared,

"I start every workday early with yoga, meditation, and a light breakfast (fruit and yogurt). Then I work until lunch, when I leave for a stroll on the beach. I then return to work until 3:30pm, quitting time. I turn my phone off, close my laptop and don't

---

[63] Cable modem, wireless router, booster, or hot spot device

think of work a minute after 3:30pm. That's the key to being as productive as I am, and not burned out."

ONLINE BANKING

Make sure your bank allows you to bill-pay, fax wire transfer information, and charges zero or minimal currency transactions fees. At the time of writing, Charles Schwab offered a High Yield Investor Checking account with no monthly service fees or minimums, no foreign transaction fees, unlimited ATM fee rebates worldwide, mobile deposits from your smartphone, and FDIC insurance up to $250,000! See *Banking* in the *Before you Leave* section for more information.

COMMUNICATION

Business would not exist without communication. Your business may require both local and international communication options.

Let's begin with phone communication. How's your internet connection? If your service is reliable and your

electricity rarely fails, then Skype and magicJack could be excellent options for an international phone solution. If you maintain international clients, you can purchase a phone number with the desired country and area code for a one time annual fee through Skype. You could then forward all of those numbers to funnel through the same phone with the use of Google Voice. If you plan to serve the Ecuadorian community then you need to have an local number, most likely a cell phone for smaller one person operations. You can also research landline options through government-owned CNT.

I purchased a San Diego area code number from Skype for $60 USD for a year subscription. In addition to a US number, I was given 3 way calling, group video conferencing, and a personal voicemail. As with any internet phone service, there are glitches from time to time. I've had a few instances where my voicemail didn't pick up, and my client was unable to leave a message, but it is a rare occurrence.

With Skype, the customer can buy a subscription for just about any type of unlimited calling they desire: North America, Latin America, and world wide all starting at $2.99 per month!

If you have a smart phone and a local sim card installed,[64] download the Skype app. Once you are logged in and have a strong connection to the internet through either cellular or wifi, you are able to use all of your Skype features on the go!

VIRTUAL ADMIN SUPPORT

There are a variety of administrative support options available virtually. Packages range from answering services to full-time virtual assistants (VAs). Answering services start at just 80¢ a day including a friendly operator answering the phone with your company's name. Afterwards,

they either forward the call or take a message then email and/or fax the message to you. ReceptionHQ has an iPhone app that allows you to change receptionist settings and diversion numbers from anywhere in the world. They offer a free seven day trial. Try them out before you leave the country and see what you think.

http://www.receptionhq.com

A virtual assistant (VA) is exactly what it sounds like, a private secretary that works from his/her home. They can answer and respond to phone calls, filter through and answer your emails, and redirect the ones that require your special attention. Common tasks also include: booking your travel, managing your personal and professional calendar, managing social media, blogging, chat room presence, and running down leads.

Tim Ferriss emphasized the usefulness of VAs in his book The 4-Hour Work Week.[65] One

---

[64] See Logistics for more information about local sim cards

[65] http://bit.ly/4hrworkweekbook

example of a VA company is EAHelp http://bit.ly/USVAs. They provide an executive assistant starting with as little as five hours a week.

MAIL

One common problem for expats is how to handle mail. Most expats maintain a US address for credit cards, government IDs, and sometimes a business address (often a family member's address). If you have someone you trust who wants to help out, then they can receive, photograph, and email your mail to you.

If not, there are private mail services that can handle your needs. They provide two addresses, one for letters and one for packages. See *Mail* in the *Before you Arrive* section for more mail services and more information.

Keep track of your mail. You are permitted to receive $500 USD of goods every six months duty free. However, there are new laws that will go into effect soon that will

charge a $42 fee to packages under 4 kilograms and $400 of value if they are not shipped using Ecuador's Correos system.

ELECTRONICS

Operating from anywhere around the world requires you to be connected, so your electronics need to reflect mobility. A laptop is much more practical than the desktop you may be accustomed to if you plan to work from a variety of locations (pool, beach, time share, hotel, etc).

In Ecuador, a cable modem is not always provided through your cable provider, so make sure you get a good one from the States.

Also, make sure you pick up a wifi router (if it's not included in your cable modem). If you're a real techie, pick up a wifi booster. The cement walls used in home construction translate to blocked wifi signal. Spend $60 USD and pick up a booster (The Almond[66] is my favorite) and your signal will

---

[66] http://amzn.to/1m2ymQ1

reach upstairs! Simply plug it in at the top of the stairs, and it will connect with the wifi from downstairs during configuration!

See the **Electronics & Techy Tips** section for more information.

TAXES, CORPS, & BANKING

Tricks for currency conversion, insights on taxes and reporting, & an introduction to Ecuadorian banking

"PAYING THE MAN"

The Ecuadorian government takes getting paid seriously. Make certain you are on time filing your corporate tax returns: April 2nd - 28th. Taxes in Ecuador are no less complex than those in North America. I highly suggest you secure a talented attorney or CPA to make sure you are paying correctly. Here is a link to a lengthy pdf that breaks down Ecuador's taxes in a hard to read dry manner: http://bit.ly/ECtaxes

In addition to annual corporate taxes, many companies are required to report monthly! Even if you didn't make a dime, you must report what you did or did not make each month. If you are just one day late, you will be fined. It gets better... because

Ecuador's IRS won't review your file until the following annual review, if you rat yourself out and fess up about the late submission your fine is halved. If you don't realize you were late filing, you will learn an expensive lesson. The government will let you know how many occurrences you were late and the corresponding fine for each infraction.

EXPAT EXPERIENCE

"I learned the hard way about the seriousness of Ecuadorian tax payments to the SRI. In 2013, I spent quite a bit of time out of the country taking care of my terminally ill mother. As a result, my monthly tax reporting was not done timely on three separate occasions. In March of 2014, I was sent certified mail from the Ecuadorian SRI with fines of $250 for each occurrence. I was infuriated, because I missed the filing date by only 4 or 5 days. If I had caught the error during the 2013 tax year, I could have auto-reported the tardiness and only incurred a $125 fine. Lesson learned!"
~ Amy Prisco, Owner of REMAX Salinas
alprisco@gmail.com

INTERNATIONAL TAX

There are a variety of proposals being thrown around worldwide to create an international tax or tax on a company/ individual's worldwide income. The provocation for change is international multi-million dollar companies including Google, Starbucks, and rich individuals who have given up their US citizenship just before receiving a large sum of money from an investment or inheritance while utilizing international shields to dodge paying taxes (hello Eduardo Saverin).

The United States and other developed countries have realized that without the proper taxation of theses mega offshore companies and rich individuals, they are loosing billions of dollars.

In 2013, the US saw more than double the number of people emigrating than any other full year in the history of the United States, over 3,000 people. This shift is believed to be due to a 2010 law entitled the Foreign Account Tax

Compliance Act (FATCA) which was implemented this year (2014). The FATCA makes it 'legal' for the US to bully financial institutions around the world into providing account numbers of clients who hold US citizenship. This information is then sent to the good ole' IRS. Read more about FATCA in the **US Tax** section.

As of this writing, there are no taxes on worldwide income. By definition, an international tax would create double taxation. If the US is successful in creating it, they will be able to add double taxation to Washington D.C.'s taxation without representation faux pa. Keep your eye on this issue if you own an international business or have assets in a foreign bank.

BUSINESS BANKING

As a business owner, you will be required to open an Ecuadorian bank account to pay taxes and manage your books. Keep the following paperwork handy:

☐ Copies of your passport

☐ Your Corporate paperwork

☐ Article of Incorporation

☐ Permits, *permisos*

☐ Copy of your lease (storefront)

Better yet, take your incorporation attorney and have him/her assist you in opening the account. Ecuadorian attorneys are often happy to lend a hand since they know the process and exactly what the bank needs. The help with Spanish is also a great asset. More than likely, the bank will be a short stroll away!

Online banking is available and widely used.

Banco Pichincha
Banco del Pacífico (BPE)
Banco de Guayaquil
Produbanco
Banco Internacional
Citibank

MOVING MONEY

Western Union

An oldie but goodie at times. Western Union cuts out the middle man and allows you to send money to people around the world.

Wire Transfer

This is the most used and simplest way to send larger sums of money into the country. Unfortunately, times are changing. The assumption is if you are moving large sums of money out of North America, especially the US, then you must be doing something naughty with it. Since FACTA[67] passed, banks are required to ask you what you're doing with *your* money as if that's any of their business!

Paypal

Paypal can be a great way to get paid for a service or product. There is an Ecuadorian Paypal, however, you must link it to a US bank account. So, if you're looking for a US-free financial solution, this isn't it. It also doesn't allow you to run Ecuadorian credit cards.

Wells Fargo

Wells Fargo has an option called "Express Send." You can wire money online from your US account to Banco De Guayaquil in Ecuador for just $9. Not only is it a great rate but it's called express for a reason, it arrives in less than an hour! In order to set up *Express Send,* you must go through a two week set up process but it's worth it! They also have an account package called the PMA package[68] that allows you two fee-free ATM withdrawals per statement

---

[67] http://www.irs.gov/Businesses/Corporations/Foreign-Account-Tax-Compliance-Act-FATCA

[68] http://bit.ly/fargoPMA

period. The PMA package has a $30 monthly fee that is waived if you maintain at least $25,000 in your account.

If you send money to an Ecuadorian Bank that's not on their "special list" then they charge the industry standard $40-$50.

US TAXES

It doesn't take a tax professional to recognize that the US wants their cut of the pie. Even though you have left the States, they will still tax you. Some expats have given up their citizenship in an effort to avoid paying taxes to a country they do not live in. If your worth is greater than $622,000 and you gave up your citizenship, you may be pursued by the IRS for tax evasion. The US has even gone so far as to create an Expatriation Tax which requires the expat who has renounced their citizenship to pay taxes for 10 years after they are no longer a US citizen!

Since the US is losing people from the highest tax brackets to other countries, they have enacted a new law to deter others from emigrating. You are no longer allowed to reacquire your citizenship once you renounce it! Seems like the government holds a grudge!

FATCA- *Foreign Account Tax Compliance Act*[69]

FATCA is a government response to heavyweight tax evaders. A provision as recent as July 1, 2014 was initiated through FATCA *requiring* foreign financial institutions with US clients to provide annual reports to the IRS with the name, address, largest account balance in the year, and total debits and credits of any account owned by their U.S. customer. The new law is a way for the United States to monitor where you are, how much money you have, and impose a 30% withholding tax for institutions concerning U.S. securities who do not comply.

[69] To read the argument why FATCA is bad for Amercia go to: http://bit.ly/FATCAbad

It's going to be a roller coaster ride watching this dramatic new law play out. Only time will tell how big of a mess we will end up in. Hundreds of international banks have closed the accounts of their US customers due to the outrageous demands by the US (FATCA).

You can file your US tax return through a U.S. Embassy or mail it.[70]

FOREIGN EARNED INCOME EXCLUSION
for US citizens

A potential break in the aggressive US tax requirements is the Foreign Earned Income Exclusion. In order to qualify, you must be a US citizen, your tax country must be outside of the US, be a "bona fide resident" of Ecuador *(or other non-US country)*, and have spent ≥330 full days there during a period of 12 consecutive months. The days are in total, they do not have to be consecutive, and are not reset on January 1st. In any

12 month span, you cannot have spent more than 34 days outside of EC to qualify.

EXPAT EXPERIENCE

"I had a US registered corporation with the name Ecuador in it, for which I had both bank accounts and credit cards issued by JP Morgan Chase bank. Chase sent out a letter stating they were closing all those accounts. When I called to question the letter, I was informed that Chase's policy was to no longer maintain accounts that had the appearance of being managed internationally.

Undoubtedly this decision by Chase is a direct result of FATCA regulation (although no one at Chase would comment to that extent). It remains to be seen if, or how, the other US banking institutions handle their account owners who reside overseas.

If capital controls of this nature come to Ecuador, many Expats who have funds here in Ecuador could possibly suffer negative repercussions. We need to watch equally the financial happenings in the US as well as Ecuador."

~Amy Prisco, owner REMAX Salinas
alprisco@gmail.com

---

[70] Go to the IRS website, U.S. Citizens and Resident Aliens Abroad section for more information.

If you qualify, you won't have to pay any taxes on income up to $97,600. You may also qualify to deduct foreign housing costs. The annual cap for the housing exclusion is $29,280 or 30% of the maximum Foreign Earned Income Exclusion. Remodeling, decorating, and furnishing is not included.

If you qualify for the exclusion, it doesn't mean you don't have to file taxes. You are required to file if you made more than $9,750 in world-wide income. You may not pay a dime, but Uncle Sam wants to keep an eye on you.

The most popular tax forms for the expat are the standard 1040, Form 2555-Foreign Earned Income Exclusion and the Form 1116- Foreign Tax credit.

The rules for this exclusion are not simple. I would recommend using a CPA or other tax professional who specializes in expatriate taxes. This section is in no way to be used as the sole reference for

tax guidance. It's simply a gringo's take on expat taxes as best I can understand. *See the resource directory for CPAs and attorneys vouched for by expats.*

FBAR
Report of Foreign Bank & Financial Accounts[71]

Any US citizen that has over $10,000 in accumulative accounts outside of the US at anytime during the calendar year is required to report it to the US government. Even if it was for the purchase of a house, and you simply transferred the money into your Ecuadorian bank account where it was immediately routed out during escrow.

The filing deadline is June 30th every year. This year (2014) was the first time it was required to file online. You will need to download free Adobe Acrobat if your computer doesn't already have it.

---

[71] http://bit.ly/FBARtax

CANADIAN TAX CONSIDERATIONS[72]

If you're Canadian and planning a move to Ecuador, the government wants you to inform the Canada Revenue Agency (CRA) before you leave to work out what your residency status will be. They have a form to help you decide what status fits your situation: NR73. Numerous Canadian expats follow the stance that they can decide what their residency status is for themselves and opt not to share information.

In order to keep your GSI (Guaranteed Income Supplement) you must pop into Canada at least once every six months. Below is a list of other deal breakers that would result in the loss of your GSI:

• You don't file an individual Income Tax and Benefit Return by April 30, or if, by the end of June each year, they have not received the information about your net income for the previous year
• You leave Canada for more than six consecutive months
• Your net income is above the maximum annual[73] income
• You are incarcerated in a federal penitentiary for two years or longer
• You die (morbid but true)

I always advise you to consult your tax professional with important decisions such as this one. Reading through governmental jargon is seemingly impossible to decipher. So if the below bullet-points leave you scratching your head or throwing this book across the room, just leave it to the professionals.

The information below covers each resident status in Canada and is quoted from a Canadian governmental website: travel.gc.ca

• **Factual residents**
  · Working temporarily outside Canada

- Teaching or attending school in another country
- Commuting (going back and forth daily or weekly) from Canada to your place of work in the United States, or
- Vacationing outside Canada

- **Deemed residents**
    * A federal, provincial or territorial government employee who was a resident of Canada just before being posted abroad or who received a representation allowance for the year
    * A member of the Canadian Forces
    * A member of the Canadian Forces oversea's school staff who chooses to file a return as a resident of Canada
    * Working under a Canada International Development Agency assistance program if you were a resident of Canada at any time during the three-month period just before you began your duties abroad
    * A dependent child of one of the four persons described above and your net income for the year was not more than the basic personal amount (line 300 in the General Income Tax and Benefit Guide) or
    * A person who, under an agreement or convention (including a tax treaty) between Canada and another country, is exempt from tax in that other country on 90% or more of their income from all sources because of their relationship to a resident (including a deemed resident) of Canada

- **Non-residents**
    * Normally or routinely live in another country and are not considered a resident of Canada
    * Do not have significant residential ties to Canada, and

* Live outside Canada throughout the tax year, or
* Stay in Canada for less than 183 days in the tax year

• **Deemed non-residents**
  * If you are a factual resident or a deemed resident of Canada and are considered to be a resident of another country that has a tax treaty with Canada, you may be considered a deemed non–resident of Canada for income tax purposes.

BRITISH PENSIONS

QROPS & QNUPS[74] are two five letter acronyms every British expat should know.

QROPS stands for Qualifying Recognized Overseas Pension Scheme, but is often called an 'offshore' pension because the providers of said pension work from financial centers around the world.

There are more than 3,000 options available across 46 countries. Some expats opt to work with a financial adviser instead of dealing directly with a QROPS provider. There are various rules and tax implications depending on the laws of the country where the program is based.

Reasons why a Brit might want to consider a QROPS include:
• up to 30% lump sum availability
• inherent tax free
• portability

QNUPS stands for Qualifying Non-UK Pension Scheme. The two programs are very similar, consult your financial advisor to decide which is better for you and your family.

---

[74] http://bit.ly/UKexpatpension

HOW TO LIVE FOR FREE

WORK TRADES AND HOUSE-SITTING

Living for free is not a myth or a gimmick. People are living rent and food free across the globe. This lifestyle is temporary for some and permanent for others! It can serve in financial hardship or offer an alternative lifestyle for folks who aren't attached to things, locations, and consumerism. It certainly pulls at the heartstrings of nomads.

Whatever the reason, whatever your situation, it's possible so unless you're attached to the idea of paying rent, it would be crazy not to consider!

HOUSE-HOTEL-PET-SITTING

Exactly as it sounds, if you are a house, hotel, or pet sitter, you watch and maintain the property and animals per the instructions of the owner. If you do your homework right, this type of arrangement is a win win and can be an excellent way to save money while experiencing life as a local in a new area!

There is a huge range of responsibilities from one sitting job to another. Which is why it's imperative to ask all of the right questions, gather all the information, rules, and expectations before you commit to a job. Your tasks could range from watching a house and watering plants, to a rigorous pet activity and care program that requires something of you every couple of hours. Below are some examples of websites that advertise care-taking jobs. While options in EC exists, none of the sites exist solely for Ecuador and their inventory constantly turns over.

• MindmyHouse.com

$20/year

• HouseCarers.com
$50/year
This site has room for improvement, but is an excellent choice for those seeking a house in the land down under

• CareTaker.org
$30/year
I have personally used this site, and find that it has extensive listings. The downside is it doesn't allow you to view all of the listings without subscribing.

• TrustedHouseSitters.com
$49 for 3 months
$64.00 for 6 months
$79.00 for 12 months
This site offers more listings than any of the others.

Word of Mouth & Part-Time Expats

Keep your eyes and ears open for opportunities to help other expats keep their home and pets safe while they visit family back home!

You will have to put forth some effort to land a house/ pet sitting gig. After all, living for free is a pretty epic goal and competition can be fierce. The first job is often the hardest to land because you lack experience and pertinent references. The key to success is to look at each sitting opportunity as a job interview. Be professional, polite, and learn as much about the position as possible before you make any decisions.

The profile you create (with the service you subscribe to) is the equivalent of your resume. If you don't put in effort here, don't bother subscribing. Remember, these home and pet owners are looking for a stranger to welcome into their home when they aren't going to be there! Don't sound like a robot, be yourself in a respectable way and show passion. Let them get to know you through your profile.

Include examples that display how responsible you are: your hobbies, your cleanliness, pet enthusiasm, experience, your hobbies, and what you can do for them. Don't just say you like dogs, make sure and use examples demonstrating how much you care for animals (i.e. you're a volunteer for a local humane society). If you have horse, gardening, or farming experience, say so. If you haven't worked as a house/ pet sitter abroad, but have done so for family and friends include those experience and offer the references. If you have experience with www.couchsurfing.org, make sure to include that along with your user name then the homeowners can read your reviews as a guest and host on the site. When in doubt, ask for previous bosses, landlords, and even teachers to vouch for your trustworthiness and reliability.

Everyone has a special set of skills, if yours happens to be handy work, then mention it. Homeowners will feel better knowing their home will be cared for if something breaks while they are away. If you have gardening skills, marketing skills, computer skills, alternative energy skills, list them. You never know how your skills could benefit the homeowner. After all, the goal here is a mutually beneficial relationship!

Once you find a job you want to apply for, you have a chance to send a brief message along with your profile for their review. Treat this message like a cover letter. A brief introduction to what you can do for them, why their house is the job you want, and why they should hire you over other prospective sitters. Make sure to be passionate and real. Show your personality in a professional way.

Speaking of professionalism, make sure to respond quickly and professionally to each email correspondence. Write their name at the top, use full sentences, and always end your message with something to the effect of, "I appreciate your time and consideration."

Hesitation may cost you excellent housesitting opportunities. If the house is in a desirable location, the position will often be filled the same day it posts. Setting up

alerts for your desired location could be the most important thing you do with your service.

Once you have captured a homeowner's interest and have answered their questions or concerns, don't neglect your own. You need to ask the right questions to insure the position is a good fit for you. Ask the owner:

• Is it ok to have guests?
• How long can the pet/house can be left alone? (You may wish to explore a nearby town for the weekend)
• Is there a vehicle you can use?
• What is public transit like near them?
• How far away is the nearest grocery store?
• Will you have access to the internet?
• Is there warm water?
• Are there any rules you need to abide by?

MASTERING SITTING

In order to be an excellent house/pet sitter, all that's

required is common sense and fullfillment of the owner's requests. Remember, you're a guest so make sure you return the home in *better* condition than you received it. Wash the linens you used, make certain the house is tidy, and if you'd like some brownie points, make some brownies! Leave something homemade in the fridge for their arrival home with a note so they know you made it especially for them.

Pay close attention to the owner's requests. If the owner asks you to leave the mail in a certain area, take care to neatly place the mail in its designated place. If they'd like you to check in via email every so often, make sure and set an alarm in your calendar to do so. If you respect their wishes and go above and beyond the minimum expectation, you will accumulate an unending list of glowing references enabling a rent-free lifestyle for as long as you'd like.

WORK EXCHANGE

A work exchange is bartering work for accomadations. It's a great opportunity to see what it's like to live and work in a new region or with a new culture without taking financial risk.

Workaway.info and Helpx.net are two great websites that allow you to search for places to work in exchange for free room and board *(On the flip side, once you decide to buy a home, you can host workers through the site to help you remodel, or advertise a new business in exchange for room and board.)*

Just like housesitting, your profile matters! Take time to construct one that really draws on your skill-set. Next, search the country where you'd like to work and the type of work that you'd like to do.

For example, I searched Ecuador and organic farm stay. This resulted is a list of organic farm owners who were looking for some extra help in exchange for room and board. The range of work possibilities is extensive. Examples of work projects include: help with new construction, marketing, refurbishing a boat, gardening, cooking, teaching English, farming, housekeeping, concierge, working with horses, etc.

The most common arrangement I've seen advertised is approximately 20 hours of work in exchange for free room and board. I'd also say that farming both organic and in-organic offer the most jobs.

Make sure and clarify your specific arrangement with the owner because every situation is unique. Some work exchanges are full-time in exchange for free room and board and an additional stipend. I've seen others that want you to pay them for some of your expenses and work full time for them.

Free room and board is great, walking away from a few months living alongside a new culture, town, way of life, with a new skill, is priceless!

The Caretakers Gazette also offers work exchanges for a small stipend and free room and board. On that particular site, I've observed work as caregiver, handy-person, and live-in hotel manager most frequently.

COUCH SURFING

Couch surfing is not just a way to describe sleeping on your cousin's couch any longer. Now, it is an entire genre of travel. People of all ages travel around the world meeting Couch Surfers from every country they've traveled.

Couch surfing is a free short-term local housing solution. The average stay is two nights. It's a great way to travel around EC searching for the region that best suits you, and gathering information and advice from locals and expats who have already made the move.

www.CouchSurfing.org is a site whose slogan is, *"Changing the world one couch at a time."* To experience this new way of travel, all you need to do is sign up and create a free profile. There, you can decide whether you'd like to host travelers, play tour guide, or simply chat over a cup of joe, and exchange stories.

You're never required to host someone, even if your profile says that you can. You can search for potential hosts, or for *surfers* looking for a place to stay in your area. If you find a "couch" you'd like to surf, simply write to them.

In your couch surfing request, tell them why you'd like to stay with them in particular. Show them that you took the time to read their profile.

Even though it's called "couch" surfing, oftentimes your host has a spare bedroom you can have all to yourself! The sleeping situation is listed in the profile of the potential host. I've couch surfed in Canada, St. Lucia, and across the United States. I have hosted surfers many times in Costa Rica and had excellent experiences making friends with travel peers around the world!

ADDITIONAL READING
- *Work Your Way Around the World: The Globetrotter's Bible* by Susan Griffith
- *The Work From Home Handbook* by Diana Fitzpatrick and Stephen Fishman

PART VI
HEALTHCARE & GOLDEN YEARS

An introduction to healthcare, supplemental insurance, retirement, & the part-time expat

HEALTHCARE

Healthcare is a big deal for most. Take a look at elections across the globe, a leading promise is always to better healthcare. Why? Because it matters. We want the assurance if we get sick and are in need of care or a life saving procedure, we will have access. In addition to a language and culture barrier, Ecuador has a health system unfamiliar to expats. So let's get familiar with it, shall we?

Healthcare is quirky and personal. Each individual's comfort level will vary. Some folks prefer to pay out of pocket and others choose to purchase a combination of public, private, and international healthcare insurances. Each plan carries a corresponding price tag and peace of mind.

PREVENTION

Below are a few Ecuadorian friendly, illness prevention techniques:

• Eat like the locals and your weight and cholesterol should see a natural drop *(i.e. soup, rice & beans, lean meat)*.

- Take daily walks through your new natural oasis and see your mood, energy level, bone density, Vitamin D levels, and health improve.
- Replace sugar drinks and beer with fresh coconut water (coco helado) and smoothies made from the ridiculously delicious produce.

VACCINATIONS

It's a good idea to go to a travel clinic or schedule an appointment with your doctor in order to discuss and receive vaccinations. The CDC recommends[75] the following vaccinations:

- Hepatitis A
- Typhoid
- Hepatitis B
- Rabies *(for those who plan to work with dogs, live in remote areas, adventure travel, or caving)*
- Yellow Fever required if entering Ecuador from Peru or Colombia *(Recommended for the following provinces east of the Andes Mountains less than 2300 m in elevation: Morona-Santiago, Napo, Orellana, Pastaza, Sucumbios, and Zamora-Chinchipe. Also reccommend for travel to the following provinces west of the Andes and less than 2300 m in elevation - Esmeraldas, Guayas, Los Rios, Manabi, and designated areas of Azuay, Bolivar, Canar, Carchi, Chimborazo, Cotopaxi, El Oro, Imbabura, Loja, Pichincha, and Tungurahua - recommended only for those at risk for a large number of mosquito bites. Not recommended for travel limited to areas greater than 2300 m in elevation, the cities of Guayaquil and Quito, or the Galápagos Islands. Required for travelers arriving from a yellow-fever-infected area in Africa or the Americas).* Just get it.

If you have any questions or other concerns about vaccinations and other health precautions (i.e. safe food, water practices, and insect bite protection) call the Centers for Disease Control and Prevention's hotline: 1-877-FYI-TRIP (1-877-394-8747).

CARE

Sometimes, the right healthcare option for you is a matter of comfort. If you've had the same cardiologist or family

---

[75] http://wwwnc.cdc.gov/travel/destinations/traveler/none/ecuador

practitioner for years, you have a history and trust that was built over the course of many years. Moving to Ecuador will reset that comfort level. In order to manage this change, I highly recommend you interview doctors during your *"try before you pry"* time. Make an appointment and interview specialists that are applicable to your needs.

INTERVIEW YOUR DOCTOR:

☐ Where did they complete schooling?

☐ Are they board certified? *(All physicians are licensed but not all are board certified.)* If so, in what specialty?

☐ How many patients have they had with my particular ailment/ condition?

☐ How can you reach them outside of office hours? Cell phone number?

☐ Do they respond to calls during office hours?

☐ If they are out of town, who fills in for them?

EXPAT EXPERIENCE

"The U.S. medical services are driven by the insurance companies. There, I was seen by my family provider, who referred me to an ENT. The ENT said I was grinding my teeth at night – referred me to a dentist (I do twice a year visits to my dentist). He immediately knew that was not the case and referred me to another ENT who stated that I needed to wear a mouth guard at night. Back to my family doctor, I get referred to get an MRI. MRI shows nothing. Back to the family doctor and 10 years of the back and forth with no results.

My experience here in Ecuador was positive; the care was spectacular. House calls are the norm at no additional cost. I got a sonogram, CAT scan (revealing a benign tumor), biopsy, pain medicine, and results (yes, that is a big deal). The cost of the whole lot was about $500. Dr. Elke speaks English; Dr. Victor is her husband. I called Dr. Elke and she did my initial visit. We then worked with Dr. Victor and Dr. Elke translated.

We used the dental services here and were pleased. It's quite simple – call and make an appointment. But, when you get to your appointment, be prepared to be seen. Not like in the states where you wait for hours. Nope, you are at 10:00, you are in the chair at 10:00."
~ Diane & Mark Bublack, expats from Houston

☐ What is their philosophy of healthcare?

☐Do they have more than one location to see patients?
☐How do they handle billing?

After you have collected all of your information with at least three physicians (preferably those you have been referred to), decide what questions and answers hold the most stout with you and score them accordingly. Don't forget to weigh in heavily with your comfort level and rapport with your future physician.

QUALITY

Quality of healthcare fluctuates greatly across the country. In larger cities like Quito, Cuenca, and Guayaquil, there are newer medical facilities[76] with great equipment and bi-lingual doctors, many of who are US board certified.

Medical care is very limited outside of Quito and Guayaquil. Basic medical services are available in many small towns and villages. However, treatment for an acute illness or utilization of specialists are often unavailable outside of Quito.

In an emergency, individuals are taken to the nearest hospital that will accept a patient. This is usually a public hospital unless the patient or someone acting on their behalf indicates that they can pay for a private hospital.

One major difference in Ecuador is private hospitals and medical practitioners require payment at the time of service or even before treatment is given. Sadly, people have died waiting for proof of payment to process.

Payment for medical services is typically done on a cash basis, although the few private hospitals will accept major credit cards for payment. Other services that require up-front payment are ambulances. They don't provide the level of care that most North Americans are accustomed to, and they require payment prior to departure.

---

[76] Watch a 2 minute clip that demonstrates the state of art medical facilities in Ecuador. Keep in mind the movie was created for medical tourism and is therefore biased. http://bit.ly/hospitalsEC

You have probably figured out by now that U.S. healthcare insurance plans are not accepted in Ecuador. Ironically, if you opt to purchase an international healthcare plan, it will often cover every country except the United States due to their outrageously inflated medical costs.

PUBLIC HEALTHCARE

Social Security Administration or **IESS**

Ecuador's current public health structure dates back to 1967. The Ministry of Public Health is in charge of creation and regulation of health programs. Their priorities are centered around communitarian health and preventive medicine.

Part of the government healthcare system was the creation of specialty hospitals: ontological, children's, psychiatric, gynecologic and maternity, opthalmologic, geriatric, and gastroenterological.

Employers and employees in Ecuador are required to pay into the IESS system. If you aren't working but are a legal resident holding a cedula, you can opt in.

You need to go to the social security office and register. Once enrolled, you will remain covered until you die. If you decide to stop paying your monthly fee, however, you will be dropped. In early 2014, the government altered the program to allow those over 65 to enroll, and include the coverage of pre-existing conditions. If you opt in, after ten years of contributions you will be eligible for an Ecuadorian retirement which is equivalent to their minimum wage (currently $340 per month).

The fee is 21.5% of the current average Ecuadorian wage. As of the writing of this book, the fee was about $70 per month.

In order to use your IESS for appointments, you must make three payments (three months), but you can use it for emergencies right away. After your three months, you simply make telephone appointments for routine care.

At any time if there is an emergency, you head to your

local hospital. Once at the ER you simply need to present your cedula and they can verify your IESS status right away. All medical care through the IESS system is free! That includes medication and routine dental!

EXPAT EXPERIENCE

We joined IESS in March this year (2014). There are a lot of opinions or rumors, and some expats don't have a lot of confidence in it. Looking into it deeper we learned that a lot of the best doctors in town were going over to IESS, and that, in fact, they were improving the system. It appealed to the residents and professionals. We needed help signing up since we don't have a command of the language yet. We took a translator to get it set up. We were together for one hour and got it all done. James has already seen his new cardiologist, had blood work done, and we've both been to the dentist!"
~ Bev & James Peterson, expats from Wisconsin.

Let's say you require a procedure that is not offered by the public hospital, you may be referred to a private hospital that can perform the needed care at no charge to you.

The government does not pay for "elective procedures" and it considers knee or hip replacement as prosthetic devices which is also not covered.

PRIVATE INSURANCE

SALUD Healthcare

Salud offers a variety of coverage from levels 1-7 ($40 - $200 cost dependent on level chosen and medical history). One is the most affordable with higher deductibles and minimal care, seven is the Cadillac of coverages with zero deductibles and access to the best clinics and hospitals.

EXAMPLE

Expat Diane Murray paid just over $200 monthly for level 7 insurance that has zero deductibles with a cancer rider and life insurance policy.

General coverage
• 80% in outpatient procedures
• To 100% hospital inpatient
• Up to 100% in intensive care
• 60% drug coverage

Extended coverage

Expanded coverage plans give you an annual per person of $160,000 coverage.

Benefits
- Treatment of metastatic cancer, heart attacks, bypass surgery, stroke, chronic renal failure, severe burns, and major organ transplant.
- Accidental involuntary death coverage.
- Coverage abroad.
- Glasses, prostheses, orthoses and for the attentions of dentistry, psychiatry and psychology, there are agreements available.
- Physiotherapeutic procedures: 10 annual sessions by the contract person.

Prices range from $75 a month to $235 depending on your age and plan selection.

OUT OF POCKET

Healthcare is cheap so some healthy folks just opt to pay out of pocket! This is a common path for younger and healthy expats. Be warned, however, I know of an expat who fell and broke his hip. All said and done, he paid over $20,000 (including surgery, treatment of anemia, physical therapy, and months of rehab).

If you are concerned about cost, feel free to call the hospital where you would go and ask them the costs of a variety of procedures. They have a fee schedule and will tell you the cost and the minimum you need to bring to get through the doors. Remember you will not be seen until you can prove payment. That fact can send those on the fence towards IESS where they know you are covered with a simple entrance of your cedula into the computer system, or private insurance where a simple confirmation phone call should do the trick.

GROUP HEALTHCARE

A growing trend is group plans. You need two main ingredients, a large group of expats in need of healthcare and a healthcare broker who can sell you a package plan with a group discount. Here[77] is a summary of a customized plan that was created for an expat community in Ecuador (March 2014):

No waiting period, no health history, no pre-existing condition exclusions!

- Maximum coverage per event of $50,000
- Deductible per year per member $120
- 100% LND coverage up to $2,200
- Emergency Medical Travel Insurance Abroad per trip (first 30 days) 100% coverage up to $10,000
- Prescription drugs 80%

Optional add on: Catastrophic Health Coverage:

- Up to $250,000 coverage per event
- $20,000 deductible (can be met by primary insurance coverage)
- Transplant organs for life 100% up to $50,000 (80% after)

Dental Option
- Maximum limit per member, per year $2,000
- Maximum limit for orthodontics per member, per year $1,000
- Dental coverage 80%

PriceTag (lowest rates in the scale quoted):
$85 per person, per month or $225 per family, per month for everything listed above!

INTERNATIONAL HEALTHCARE

There is a growing trend towards international lifestyles. If you don't plan to live in any one place full time or you travel so much you're barely at home, an international plan might be a better option for you.

Make sure the coverage that you choose has coverage inside the US if you think you may need to return within the given time period. Many insurances omit the US due to the inflated healthcare expenses.

---

[77] http://bit.ly/echealthplan

BROKERFISH

www.brokerfish.com

This is a search option that you can use just like searching for airfare or car insurance. You enter in the ages of your family members and your desired international coverage. The most expensive factors seem to be whether or not you wish to have coverage in the US and whether or not you want to include emergency evacuation.

TRAVEL INSURANCE

If you don't plan to "stay put" for longer than 6 months at any given time then travel insurance may be your best option. An added bonus to purchasing travel insurance is besides coverage for your own flesh and bones, you can opt for insurance against lost luggage, trip cancellation, and sometimes theft! It also might be an ideal option for the part-time expat, see more in the *Part Time Expat* section.

MEDEX

www.medexassist.com

I asked for a quote for two US citizen travelers ages 64 and 50 set to travel to Ecuador for exactly 5 months. The cost for each of them was $517 for five months coverage, totaling $1,034 for their stay in Ecuador. What do you get for your money?

• Up to $250,000 coverage
• $100 deductible per incident
• Includes medical evacuation and repatriation
• Includes accidental death and dismemberment
• Coverage for controlled pre-existing conditions
• 71 and under
• No hazardous sports coverage
• Trip cancellation coverage
• To see a full outline of coverage see: http://bit.ly/medexti

DELAMORA & ASSOCIATES

The best benefit from this insurance option is *direct payment* from anywhere in the world. You won't need to deal with the hassles of reimbursement policies, or policies that force you to operate within a given medical network. They offer four different policies that can be issued for as little as one day or, in some cases, as much as 365 days. They issue consecutive vouchers if a client needs coverage for longer than 120 days.

The option of purchasing single day plans when you know you will doing something that is stupid risky such as: rock climbing, mountain biking, or driving with me is a great addition. For more information, the breakdown of coverage is online[78]
mkeller@delamorayasociados.com.mx

PHARMACIES

The pharmacy system in Ecuador is much more fluid than in the states. If you are on blood pressure, heart, or diabetic medication, you simply bring in the bottle and they will find your medicine. You don't need to present a prescription. Also, if you get an ear infection from overindulging in the ocean or pool, you can just head to the pharmacy and get the necessary antibiotics. No need to waste money and time seeing a physician for such things.

Farmacías are widely available and seen at every major corner. If you get traveler's belly or wish to take anti-parasite medicine, no problem, pop in and ask.

MALPRACTICE

Potential expats are often nervous about medical care that doesn't have the backing of a billion dollar medical malpractice insurance industry. After all, there is always risk involved with medical care, and if human error was made then it would be nice if your loved ones were covered.

There has been a shake-up since January 2014 due to new wording in Article 146, of Ecuadorian Law.

---

[78] http://bit.ly/delamorabreakdown

"The person who violates a citizen's rights through the exercise or practice of his profession, and causes someone's death, will be sanctioned with a term of imprisonment from one to three years . . . if death is the result of unnecessary, dangerous, and illegitimate actions."

The vagueness of *illegitimate actions* has been attacked by doctors worried about facing one to three years jail time if they make a mistake! They have organized numerous protests including a daily walk out around 10am in numerous hospitals countrywide.

In late April (2014), an Ecuadorian court justice clarified the article by stating,

"The professional must violate the objective duty of care is set. This offense would be configured for breach of laws, regulations, manuals, as well as lack of training and lack of diligence."

AVAILABILITY

I cannot make an all inclusive statement regarding wait times. Each region, each facility, is different. Each day a facility could have drastically different wait times from the next. Expats that I have spoken with have indicated that it was easy to see their primary care doctor, cardiologist, have blood work drawn, and so on. However, I was not able to find an expat that needed a surgery or procedure through the IESS. Diane mentioned earlier in the Private Healthcare section that she experienced superior care in Ecuador than in the US with the diagnoses and care of a benign tumor.

MEDICAL TOURISM

Three per cent of the *world*'s population travels internationally for medical treatment![79] That's roughly 211,710,000 people! Patients Beyond Borders, an organization that publishes international medical travel guidebooks, reported that the medical tourism industry produces $40 billion a year in business.

Patients requiring elective, non-elective, and dental procedures are heading to Ecuador. Procedures are often

---

[79] IPK International Survey

less than half the cost in the United States.

The medical tourism industry capitalizes where the US lacks. Companies like:
• Find Health in Ecuador[80]
• Med Travel Ecuador[81]
offer numerous cosmetic and medical procedures for a fraction of the cost in the U.S. The latter will also make your travel arrangements and their VIP services will take you by hand to everywhere you need to be.

EMERGENCIES #s

Emergency phone numbers in Ecuador vary by region. In Quito and Ibarra, dial 911 for all emergencies. In Guayaquil, Cuenca and Loja, the number is 112. Elsewhere, dial 101 for police, 102 for firefighters or ambulance, or 131 for the local Red Cross. Operators typically speak Spanish only. Physicians and hospital personnel frequently do not speak English and medical reports are written in Spanish.

Patients must have good Spanish language skills to utilize local medical resources.

Local Hospitals and Clinics

The US Embassy recommends that medical emergencies in Quito be treated at Hospital Metropolitano and Hospital De los Valles in Cumbaya. In Guayaquil, the Consulate recommends using the Clinica Kennedy and the Clinica Alcivar. Travelers are directed to these facilities because they are modern and and more technologically advanced than others in the area.

Metropolitano Hospital
Av. Mariana de Jesús s/n y Nicolás Arteta
+593-2-399-8000 Ext. 2193

Hospital De Los Valles Cumbaya
Av. Interoceanica Km. 12 ½, Cumbaya
+593-2-600-0911

---

[80] bit.ly/healthinecuador

[81] bit.ly/medtravelec

Clinica Kennedy

Av. San Jorge entre la Novena y la Decima (close to Polycentro Mall)

+593-4-228-6963 / 2289-666 and Fax: +593-4-228-4051

Clinica Kennedy (Alborada area)

+593-4-224-7900

Clinica Kennedy (Samborondon area)

+593-4-209-0039

Clinica Alcivar (Trauma specialty)

Doctora Ma del Carmen Escolano, cell phone +593-9-948-0305

Doctor Marlon Alarcon, cell phone +593-9-961-5960

BOOKS

Patients Without Borders: Everybody's Guide to Affordable, World-Class Healthcare[82]

---

[82] http://bit.ly/guidetohealthcare

RETIRED LIFE

REINVENTING YOU, GETTING CONNECTED, FALLING BACK IN LOVE WITH LIFE

Live in a place where as your age increases so does your level of respect from the community.

One size does not fit all, nor does one way of retiring fit every retired individual. This transition is not to be taken lightly. Just as your transition into adolescence, adulthood, and possibly parenthood were taken seriously so too should your transition into your wisest stage.

When considering a move to another country, you are in an ideal time to sit and reevaluate the person that you are today.

Your life experiences have shaped you and groomed you to be who you are, don't base your decisions on the person you were in the 60s, 70s, or 80s. Instead, decide what is important to you now, and what do you want to be important to you now? Reshape your life based on your answers. Moving abroad gives you a unique gift, a reset button to recreate yourself. Don't waste it!

EXPAT EXPERIENCE

I was forced to retire when our house sold in three hours. We were on a fast track to Ecuador and retirement. When we arrived in Ecuador, we were completely exhausted.

We experienced retirement together for the first time in a two bedroom apartment and a new strange culture. All of the other stuff you have to deal with in an international move is minor compared to the adjustment of retirement. Jim was used to being his own person doing whatever he wanted to do, now I'm home. I don't think that we had time to even think about it before we left. It took some time to adjust. People always underestimate the transition into retirement, it takes work."

~ Bev Petersen, expat from Wisconsin

EXPAT EXPERIENCES

Here is a brief excerpt of an email sent from late Darvin Wilson to some friends in the US:

"Actually, I changed my Thanksgiving to June 4th. That's the day I arrived in Ecuador. We had spaghetti and worked around the house and hung out by the sea. It was just another wonderful day in Salinas, the Blue Paradise of the Pacific.

A lot of, so called, expats went down to a local bar to celebrate Thanksgiving and blow smoke up each other's ass about what a great country they left. If it was so great, I don't know why they would have left."

~ Late Darvin, *Old Man*, Wilson

PRIORITIES

Homework time! Create a priority chart, listing no fewer than 15 priorities. Next to each priority, rate its importance with a 1 - 10 ranking, one representing the highest importance, ten representing the least. Some examples of priorities include: health, relationship, learning, location, spirituality, hobbies, financial security, travel, being active, giving back to the community, and family. Make a conscious effort to demonstrate your top ten priorities through time allocation.

After you have your core ten priorities, write down what success looks like in each one. For example, for health you could write: "Walk 3 miles every morning, attend yoga 2x weekly, and journal 4x weekly." This task will provide you with a way to measure your success.

Some of you may have lived for financial achievement and success, climbing the corporate ladder to the rooftop deck. You may feel a strong challenge to reshape what success looks like to you in this new stage of your life. You might not have support staff, meetings, and other daily procedures that create a sense of importance and success.

LEARN

You can't teach an old dog a new trick... Bullshit! Learn a new skill that you've always wanted to learn. Take up fly-fishing, birding, woodworking, basket weaving, hiking, or walking. Maybe you already have a few solid hobbies, take them to the next level. Buy that table saw or tool that you need to take your woodworking to the next level, or a sewing machine, new rod, or GPS device. Read a book on how to further expand your skills, watch YouTube tutorials or best yet, find an apprenticeship.

WHAT TO DO

You finally made it to retirement. Talk about the ultimate hurry up and wait. For most people, lounging by the pool all day sipping on piña coladas will be spectacular for about a week, then what? Hobbies only get you so far. What can you do that will give your life purpose? You could seek out volunteer opportunities within the community or a field of interest. Or you could pick up a part-time job.

It has become more and more common to see "retired" folks working part-time or stepping into the entrepreneur world by starting up a business they always dreamed about.

Think about projects that would be fun. Look into part-time opportunities helping local businesses in your area through consulting or independent contractor work.

Get connected through social networks near you, both expat and Ecuadorian. Try not to isolate yourself into the expat world, you miss out on so much of what Ecuador has to offer. Invite your Ecuadorian neighbors over for dinner once a month, start up, or attend a "Sunday Funday" with your gringo community.

Travel and explore your new country. There are rivers, waterfalls, forest, jungles to be seen! Don't watch them on the Discovery Channel, go out and find your passion.

When in doubt, give it time. For many it can take up to three years to fully adjust to a new culture. You have a lot of new adjustments: schedule, climate, latitude, culture, language, surroundings, activities, expectations, and so on.

If you find yourself growing disgruntled, take a "time out" and evaluate why. If you are resenting something that is and always was Ecuador, try to change your perception and appreciate Ecuador for what it is. Your new mantras could very well be: "I'm no longer in a rush", "Just roll with it," and "Look around, I'm in Ecuador, who cares if the ____ takes forever!"

HEALTHY LIVING

In Ecuador, they don't need shows like the Biggest Loser, why? Because they have high quality affordable fruit, vegetables, rice, and beans served in place of burgers and fries.

Plus, it's hard not to be at least a little bit active in Ecuador. There are many gorgeous trails and empty beaches to explore by foot, and if you're in the Sierra, everywhere is uphill both ways!

The biggest challenge to maintaining a healthy lifestyle in Ecuador is monitoring your alcohol intake.

LANGUAGE BARRIER

For those of you who are fluent in Spanish, all the rest of us are jealous!

Tips for learning Spanish:

For many adults, a major factor that slows down their language acquisition is fear of making mistakes. You didn't hear this from me but, a slight buzz can really lubricate the tongue and ease the perfectionism in you. It can also provide the liquid bravery needed to break through your learning plateaus. Too much alcohol and you can refer back to the previous section.

Picture a toddler learning English. They don't expect to get it right, so neither should the adult learner of a second language. They look adorable saying things wrong and you understand them. That will be you for awhile, an adorable gringo who is trying. More power to you!

LOVE LIFE

It's easy to fall into complacency, aiming at just surviving in life. Make a focused effort to rid your complacent habits and thrive, not survive! Experience each moment and appreciate what life is offering you in the now. Fall into love with life again. Just as a relationship has to be watered time and time again to keep it fresh and alive, so too does your soul and outlook on life.

If you are single in Ecuador, there is no reason why your perfect match isn't waiting for you in the next café. I am proof of this sentiment! I met my Utah born wife in Costa Rica! You really never know where you will meet that special someone.

It's never too late for love either! My favorite Canadians met in her 50s and his 60s, married, and couldn't be more in love! They no longer have to find a partner to sail, kayak, paddle, explore the world, and love life with!

EXPEL THE MONSTERS

Yes, Ecuador has robberies. Yes, Ecuador has both good and bad people including scam artists. What country doesn't? In the US, police will respond when you call them and will usually comply with a report and attempt to find the wrong-doer. In Ecuador, I wouldn't say I place much faith in their "investigative work." I could choose to dwell on the worse case scenarios living in Ecuador, but why would I do that? Who would it serve? I could do that

in the States and be left with rape, murder, terrorism, and mass killings.

Constant worrying will leave you in a place of fear with a victim's mentality, and could potentially drive away quality people. It will lead you down a lonely path, potentially creating a self-fulfilling prophesy.

Most Common Fears in Your Golden Years:

• You will outlive your money
• You will lose your marbles
• You will spend your last years alone

Take action with something you are passionate about as a direct rebuttal to fear. Taking action is the opposite of being a victim.

YOUR BETTER HALF

"I won't let him retire because then he'd drive me crazy!" I can't tell you how many times I have heard this from wives and husbands quoting why they can't retire (especially when I worked at a fire station). There are other options.

- Share at least one daily enthusiasm *(bird watching, cooking, volunteering, walking, swimming, kayaking, tennis, etc)*

- Keep yourselves in good shape
- Take responsibility for your own happiness
- Let go of old arguments

Recommended Books:
- *65 things to Do When You Retire* [83]
- *The Retiring Mind*,[84] Robert Delamontagne
- *The Couples Retirement Puzzle: 10 Must-Have Conversations for Transitioning to the Second half of Life*[85] Robert Taylor and Dorian Mintzer
- *Aging Bravely, Shut Up and Stop Your Whining*[86] by Dana Racinskas

---

[83] http://bit.ly/65tdretire

[84] http://bit.ly/retiringmind

[85] http://bit.ly/coupleconversations

[86] http://bit.ly/agingbravely

THE PART-TIME EXPAT

YOU'RE NOT QUITE READY FOR THE PLUNGE BUT WOULD LIKE TO DABBLE A FOOT IN?
SPECIAL CONSIDERATIONS FOR SEASONAL EXPATS

Does selling your home, your car, all of your belongings, kissing your kids and grandkids goodbye, and shipping out to Ecuador forever sound too drastic for you? It may seem impossible for you to live far from your family.

There is a middle ground. If you're a parent or grandparent, there is a good chance you have lived much of your life based around other's needs and desires. Now that your kids have kids, it's easy to get swallowed up into full-time child care and more responsibilities than you had imagined for *YOUR* golden years.

The choice is yours. If you decide you are going to chase your dreams then clearly define them and see where your family fits. If living in Ecuador full-time is too much awayness, then how about snow-birding, or halftime? Where is your balance? How long is the flight to your ideal location from your loved ones? Are there direct flights from the city where your children and grandchildren reside?

$$ LIFESTYLE

Can you afford the lifestyle you desire where you currently live on your retirement budget? If the answer is no, then ask yourself if you lived in an area of Ecuador half of the year with more luxuries for less money would that help you fill the gap in your lifestyle goals?

Do you strive for continuity? For your six months abroad, will you want to return to Ecuador each time or do you think you will want the freedom to explore other affordable countries in the years to come? Say Thailand?

THE BALANCING ACT

Living in more than one location is inherently more work. There are double the utilities to turn on, off, and manage. If you rent out one or both of your homes, then you add an additional depth of complexity. Decorating, stocking, and maintaining homes in two countries can prove exhausting. In the end, most things worth doing are difficult. Living outside the box, in two boxes rather, may be the best arrangement for you and yours. Organization and planning are key components to help tame the additional responsibilities.

Good friends of mine, Lisa and Junior, have the goal of living a third of the year across three properties: their lake house in Virginia, their beach front estate in Roatan, and are currently looking for their third spot (potentially in Ecuador). They plan to rent each property while they are away, creating a passive income while living their dream. They have it figured out!

PROPERTY MANAGEMENT

For those who opt to purchase homes, rental income can be an excellent option. Vacation rentals have helped part-time expats to minimize costs and, in some cases, make handsome profits! Ecuador's tourism industry is on the rise. The government is putting big bucks into the industry attempting to shift some focus from the unreliable oil industry.

HOUSE-SITTERS

As homeowners, you are on the flip side of those who are living rent free! You can access the same sites mentioned before in the *Living for Free* section as a homeowner seeking a house-sitter. A house-sitter is helpful for your piece of mind, and to keep your home from attracting thieves, squatters, and other problematic situations.

If you live along the coast or in the jungle, the humidity can literally rot parts of the house if it's left unused. Rust and mold may destroy your appliances, AC units, or the woodwork in your home.

TIP

If you're planning to leave for more than a day or two, I've had the best luck avoiding mold and musty odors by leaving the cabinets open, the ceiling fans on low, and the windows open. Also, if you're gone for an extended period, and plan to turn off the refrigerator, leave it open.

TRAVEL INSURANCE

If you spend no more than 6 months in one location at a time then purchasing travel insurance may be the best option for you. For more information see the *Healthcare* section.

THE MOVING BLUES

"Accept that in the first few months you may be brought to tears by the most innocuous of things. This doesn't mean you are going mad or failing; it's just part of the journey of adjustment to massive change. Cry when you need to then be determined to make the best of the next day."
~ Johanna: Irish Nomad in Malaysia

There are expats that have grown bitter and disgruntled. The most common cause is hyper-fixation on differences and change. They're like salmon, they flow along with all of the excitement and arrive to fertile EC and the party is on! Shortly thereafter, they realize it is not what they thought it would be and flip a 180. They swim upstream fighting the way things are, and fighting the nature of EC that once attracted them. They are left exhausted and eventually caught, and served for dinner.

In order to have a healthy relationship, you must love your partner for exactly the person they are today with their faults, their gifts, and everything in-between. So too, you must appreciate EC for exactly what it is today in order to live a healthy and happy life here.

I'm hopping off of my soap box now...

In every move I've made, I experienced a roller coaster of emotions. If you plan for it, it can take the edge off *a little*. Expect to have an initial high followed by an intense low. The low is mostly due to loneliness, culture shock which will be discussed next, and inaccurate expectations.

Change causes stress no matter what kind of stress it is. Moving to an amazing country that fits you perfectly is still a stressful event. There are concerns you will have and worries of endless logistics: shipping your car, container, luggage, pets, new house, new area, language acquisition, new foods, access to utilities, etc.

A key method for quick acclimation is to go out and make friends in the community. Find out the inner workings of the community and how you can contribute! If you spend all day interacting with those you left back home on Skype or magicJack then you've only left

in body and are cheating your experience.

CULTURE SHOCK

This is not a phenomena that happens to the weak. It can slug you in the face or slowly tighten around you like a boa constrictor! Merriam - Webster describes culture shock as, "A sense of confusion and uncertainty sometimes with feelings of anxiety that may affect people exposed to an alien culture or environment without adequate preparation."

There are four stages of culture shock, much like grief.

• Honeymoon phase
• Negotiation phase
• Adjustment phase
• Mastery phase

Honeymoon Phase

The honeymoon phase is the high I mentioned earlier. No wrong could be done to you or by you. You're romanticized by the differences in the culture, pace, way of life, and new exotic foods. Just like the honeymoon phase in a new relationship, you are blinded to any faults of your lover's. Not until the dust settles does their obnoxious habits start to crawl under your skin, and you see the real them.

When your electricity goes out in a storm, or your water gets shut off for a day or two, or you are overcharged for a service and you can't get anyone to help fix it, those not-so-sexy parts of Ecuador sneak up and bite you. Like I mentioned in the introduction:

"Ecuador is the land of liberties, freedom, and nature. On the flip side of those liberties exist disorganization, latency, and inefficiency. The side that you choose to focus on will directly relate to your happiness and overall experience living in this tropical wonderland."

Negotiation Phase

This is when reality settles in. When you sit down and wonder what have you done? All of the differences initially seen as romantic are all of the sudden cause for great concern. Can you really do this? Can you adjust to so many differences?

You realize how incredibly far away you are from "home" and your family. Maybe you don't know a soul in Ecuador. If you aren't fluent in Spanish, that carries with it an invisible wall. While you can't see the wall, you feel it in every interaction. You feel it when you have trouble ordering meat at the butcher counter, or paying your water bill, finding the sugar in the supermarket, or asking the bus driver how much is the fare. Additionally, it can be hard to adjust to the tropical climate (beach goers) and new food.

This phase is not pleasant and those who successfully navigate through it are gentle and patient with themselves. They also laugh at their mistakes, learn from others, and resolve that they are no longer in a hurry and no longer in the US. They learn and adopt realistic expectations.

Adjustment Phase

During this phase you have become accustomed to some of the new changes, like how long it takes to get your food while eating out and the long lines at the bank. You no longer fight the changes, you become accepting and build your routine around them. The changes become your new normal. Your understanding of the culture becomes more in-depth here, and you begin to cultivate connections with the community.

Mastery Phase

You feel 100% comfortable in your new culture. You accept the practices and participate in many aspects of the culture. You may not completely lose your culture of origin, but you are now an expert in the Ecuadorian way. You can navigate through any hurdle or problem as they arise knowing the appropriate course of action. You are ready to take a new expat under your wing and pass forward the experiences

and knowledge that countless expats gave to you.

EXPAT EXPERIENCE

"I just told Mark yesterday morning. One of the hardest things for me here was the way that expats will screw over another expat in a heartbeat. You don't trust most gringos here. They are here for a fast buck or to screw someone. Amy Prisco is one I trust. She is welcome any day of the week. Especially in construction or service, it's the expats that are rude to other expats. I'm not really good with the expats. Mark and I do not attend any of the expat functions. We are not tight knit community type of people. But then again we never were. We lived in the same neighborhood for 7 years, and I knew the names of two neighbors."
~ Diane Bublack, expat from West Virginia

TIP

Remember, being an expat is not a race or a competition. It doesn't matter if you've lived in EC for 16 years and your new friend has only been here for one. It seems like many expats want to pull out a measuring stick so they can find their place in the pecking order. Focus instead on what you have in common and enjoy each other's company.

HANDY STREET SPANISH

START OFF "IN THE KNOW" WITH SOME HIP SLANG WORDS IN ADDITION TO NECESSARY PHRASES WHEN LIVING ABROAD

SLANG

- **Much Appreciated** - muy amable
- **It's fine** - Esta Pleno
- **Really good** - buenaso
- **Jokes** - chachos
- **Party** - farra
- **I'm broke**- estoy chira
- **I have the face of a gringo?** (Are you trying to rip me off?) - Me ves la cara de gringo?
- **Geez, it's freaking cold!** - Achachai
- **Cool** - Chévere
- **Cool** - Bacán
- **Huge** - grandote
- **Dude** - tipo
- **What's new** - que hay de novedades?
- **Really delicious** - ricazo
- **Mariposa**- Gay man

- Unbelievable (literally a lie but used to mean it's incredible) - mentira
- Hook up - vacilar
- To score in the biblical sense - tirar (literally means to throw)
- Bullshit - huevada
- Space filler, I mean, that is.. - osea
- Best bud - pana
- Help out - acolitar
- Understand, to get it - cachar
- Good heavens - chuta

RESTAURANT

- The check please - la cuenta por favor
- Can I have? - Podría tener
- That's all - es todo
- Do you take credit cards? ¿Usted toma tarjetas?
- Tap water (water of the house) - Agua de la casa
- What desserts do you have? ¿Que postres tiene?
- Without onion- sin cebollas

SHOPPING/ BARGAINING

- How much - Cuanto cuesta
- What is your best price? ¿Cuánto es el ultimo?

FUELING UP

- Full, please - lleno, por favor
- Can you change the oil? - ¿Puedes cambio el aceite?
- Asking them to check the fluid levels - ¿Se puede revisar los liquidos?

PAYING THE UTILITIES

- I need to pay the electric - Necesito pagar la luz
- I'd like to recharge this number (Cell phone #) - Me gustaria recargar
- I'd like to pay ____ account number - Me gustaría pagar cuenta numero (account number, use for paying water bill).

OPENING UP A NEW CELL PHONE ACCOUNT

- I need a new prepaid account for my iPhone please - Necesito una cuenta prepago nueva para mi iPhone por favor
- Yes, I do have my passport - Sí, yo tengo mi pasaporte
- I'd like to put $20 on the account - me gustaría pagar vente doláres a la cuenta.

MECHANICAL PROBLEMS

- My brakes don't work - No funcionan los frenos
- My lights don't work - No funcionan las luces
- Every time I hit a bump my radio turns off - cada vez que me doy con un hueco se apaga la radio
- It won't start - no prende
- The battery is dead - La batería está muerta
- It makes a high pitched sound - Tiene un sonido agudo

- I ran out of gas - Me quedé sin gasolina
- The car needs an oil change - El carro necesita un cambio de aceite
- Is that part important? - ¿Es parte es importante?
- Can you repair my tire? - ¿Se puede reparar la llanta?

HOUSE REPAIRS

- Screws - Tornillos
- Nails - clavo
- Hammer - martillo
- Glue - pegamento
- Plaster - yeso
- Extension chord - cuerda de extensión
- Rope - cuerda
- Chain - cadena
- Tile - azulejo
- Pipe - tubo

LOOKING FOR A PLACE TO RENT

- Does the price include utilities? - ¿El precio incluye las expensas?
- Is there internet? - ¿Hay internet?
- Hot water? - Agua caliente

- **Air conditioning?** - Aire acondicionado
- **How does the water get to the house?** - ¿Como llega agua a la casa?

LOOKING FOR A PLACE TO BUY

- **Do you know anyone who is selling their house in the area?** - ¿Conoces a alguien que está vendiendo su casa en la zona?
- **Are there problems with the plumbing?** - ¿Hay problemas de gasfitería?
- **What is the lowest price that you will take?** - ¿Cuánto es el ultimo?
- **How does the house receive water?** - ¿De qué manera la casa recibe agua?

PURCHASING A CAR

- **How many kilometers are on it?** - ¿Cuántos kilometros tiene?
- **What year is it?** - ¿De qué año es?

- **Is the Placa clear? Show me** - ¿Estan en regla los papeles/ la placa? Muéstrame
- **What problems has the vehicle had?** - ¿Qué problemas ha tenido el vehículo?
- **Has the car been in any accidents?** - ¿El carro ha estado en algún accidente?

INTERVIEWING SCHOOLS

- **What is the school's accreditation?** - ¿Que es la acreditación de la escuela?-
- **How many students go on to attend college?** - Cuántos de los graduados asisten a la Universidad?
- **How much is the tuition?** - ¿Cuánto es la cuota?
- **What other expenses can we expect?** - ¿Qué otros gastos se puede esperar?
- **What activities does the school offer?**- ¿Qué actividades ofrece la escuela?

MEDICAL Spanish

- **I have pain in my ear -** Tengo dolor en mi oído
- **I can't hear anything -** No puedo escuchar nada
- **It hurts when I move my mouth -** me duele cuando me muevo mi boca
- **My stomach hurts -** Me duele el estómago
- **I'm allergic to Aspirin -** Soy alérgico a Aspirina
- **I'm pregnant -** Estoy embarazada
- **I have diarrhea-** Yo Tengo diarrea
- **I can't breath-** No puedo respirar!
- **I have chest pain-** Tengo dolor en el pecho
- **It started when I was walking-** Todo comenzó cuando yo estaba caminando

EXPAT ADVICE & RANDOM OBSERVATIONS

WHAT EXPATS WISH THEY WERE TOLD BEFORE THEY SHIPPED OUT

Every single expat interviewed gave the advice to rent for a year before you buy and before you make the move permanent.

AMY PRISCO, NEW YORKER TURNED ECUADORIAN

• Get to know the entire country before settling down; travel options are abundant and cheap.
• Do your homework; ask questions no matter how stupid they may seem.
• Manage your expectations – you're not in Kansas anymore.
• Roll with the punches and remember mañana doesn't necessarily mean tomorrow, it just means not today.
• Learn to find substitutes for what you thought you couldn't live without.
• Ecuadorians will ask you for color copies of your ID wherever you go, even if you've already given them a copy in the past (I should have opened up a copier business).

•Spanish language skills are important – do not expect everyone to speak English.

•When you chose to Expatriate, you cannot expect your home country's government to bail you out; make sure you are prepared for any type of possible scenario.

•Having employees can be quite challenging; make sure you know the laws as they apply to you and your situation.

•When an Ecuadorian says "sí, sí, sí" three times in a row really fast – that is another way for them to say NO.

•Ecuadorians don't know how to say NO. So, instead of telling you that they can't make it on time, they just won't show up.

•Speaking of not being on time: if you can't handle tardiness, then Ecuador may just not be the place for you...adapt, assimilate, adjust.

CONNIE WILSON, HOUSTON, TEXAS GAL TURNED ECUADORIAN

Observations:
• We don't see open sewers like we did in Nicaragua.
• Yes, there are beggars and street vendors, but they are polite. If you tell them no, they usually continue on their way.
• Yes, there are areas that are very poor but we are not seeing as much graffiti here as in Nicaragua. They have a lot of anti-drug billboards and posters.
• The fruits and veggies are fabulous.
• The police are mostly women on foot in pairs. They smile and wave and pose for crazy gringo tourists.
• So far the weather has been very nice with no need for a/c. I am sure there will be times we will need a/c, but it is a much milder climate than in Houston (between 73 - 83 F).
• The ocean water is very clear and about 70 degrees. FABULOUS!
• $2.50 gets you a good lunch of soup, fried fish, rice, plantains and a soda or juice. That includes tax and tip usually.
• $5.00 bought us a lot of fresh fruits and veggies. If you try to buy much more than that, the bag gets too heavy to carry home.

Diane Bublack, expat from West Virginia

- Do your research, know what you want, understand the risks involved, and be flexible.
- Read the Expat forums, ask questions, get involved before you move.
- Think a bit outside of your box, but please leave your nasty attitudes at home.
- Do not get caught up in the playground games like so many expatriates.
- Treat the locals with respect – you are in their homeland.
- Know who the experts are – do not think that because an individual has been through the visa/cedula process they know what they are doing. This is not the case; the process/requirements, etc., change and Dana stays on top of it; she has a great rapport with the local offices. This is a huge deal!
- Want to buy land/real estate – Amy Prisco
- Want to get a cedula or visa – Dana Cameron
- Turn off *International House Hunters* – Candy Land does not exist. Many of the people who starred on the show returned to the States within just a few months of living here (right here in Puerto Cayo).
- Bring beddings, linens, appliances, kitchen gadgets, and electronics (expensive and poor quality here).
- Get involved in your community.
- Bring your sense of humor! (GREAT ADVICE)

Bev & James Petersen, expats from Wisconsin

- Give yourself *time* to get adjusted and realize that even if you think you are not going to act like a North American, you will because that is the way you are wired.
- It's going to take *time*.
- There is very little stress in Ecuadorians, Westerners are very stressed. Try to transition and unwind.
- Don't expect to make Ecuador North America. Come and observe, appreciate the people, and learn how to slip into their civilization as best as possible.
- Be open to learning from the people and the culture.

PACKING TIPS

Plates and Flat China

Begin with the larger items. Smaller items can go toward the top. Wrap each piece individually with several pieces of newsprint. Next, wrap three to five previously wrapped plates together and stand each bundle on its edge. Never lay plates flat. Add 3-4 inches of crumpled paper and a cardboard divider before creating a second level.

Glassware and Crystal

Always individually wrap each glass and never put one piece inside another. Place on the very top level of your carton and pack rim down. Especially fragile items should be packed in a separate carton and then packed in a larger carton surrounded by cushioning.

Bowls

Wrap individually and then nest two to three together and wrap as an entire package. Place on end or flat. Use crumpled paper and a cardboard divider before adding layers.

Lamps

Remove shade, bulb and harp assembly. Double wrap the bulb and harp assembly. Wrap the base and cushion it in a dish pack or similar type box. For lampshades, select the carton size close to the shade measurements. Pack only one shade per container. Don't use crumpled newsprint inside or around the outside of the shade. Glass lampshades and chandeliers should be professionally packed in sturdy crates.

Food

Of course, never pack perishable items, aerosol kitchen products or frozen food. Box dry foods in medium-sized cartons after taping any openings or tops closed. Jars should be also taped shut and wrapped as well as cushioned. Pack cans and jars in smaller cartons.

Clothing

Clothing can be left in sturdy dressers or packed in suitcases, if desired. Other foldable clothing should be packed in medium-sized cartons. Hanging clothing should be packed in wardrobe cartons. If wardrobe cartons are not used, be sure to remove hangers and pack in lined cartons. Hats should be left in their boxes and packed in moving cartons. Small boxes loosely filled with newsprint also help protect hats.

Mirrors, Glass Table Tops, Pictures, Paintings, etc.

We recommend purchasing special boxes for all but the smallest items in this category. Mirror and picture cartons can handle most items. Only one article should be packed in each carton. You will want to consider professional crating assistance for oversized or heavy items such as table tops.

Glasses and Cups

Wrap individually. Cups with handles should be cushioned with another layer of paper. Pack with rims down. Cushion and layer with crumpled paper.

Books

Pack in smaller boxes with open edges alternating with the bindings. Hardcover books, or those with fragile covers should be wrapped for protection.

Draperies and Curtains

Wardrobe cartons are excellent for hanging curtains and drapes. You can also fold them and pack in boxes that have been lined with clean newsprint.

Bedding

Mattresses must be covered to protect them from soil and damage. Appropriate sized cartons are recommended.

Small Appliances

Clocks, radios and other small appliances should be individually wrapped and packed along with linens and towels or surrounded with crushed paper for protection.

Flowers and Plants

Artificial flower arrangements should be carefully wrapped and packed in individual cartons. If possible, secure the arrangement to the bottom of the box. Cushion and label appropriately.

Electronics and Clocks

Original manufacturers packaging with Styrofoam inserts provides the best protection for moving electronic goods. If these are not available, large or medium cartons should be used and the item well wrapped and cushioned. Larger home electronics such as consoles and large screen TVs should not be packed and will be moved as furniture. Computers and grandfather clocks require special pre-move preparation.

Washing Machines

Washing machines should have all hoses disconnected and put into containers. If you place hoses in the tub or drum, be sure to wrap the metal couplings with cloth or paper to avoid damage to the tub's surface. Unplug the electric cord and tape to the back. Secure the washer drum.

Refrigerators

Refrigerators should be emptied of all food. Shelves should be secured in place or detached and wrapped. The electric cord should be unplugged and taped to the back. If there is an icemaker, it should be disconnected from the water line and drained.

Tools

Any power tools containing gasoline or oil should be drained before moving. Gas tanks can be cleaned with brake cleaner. Long handled tools can be bundled then wrapped. Hand tools should be wrapped and packed.

* *Packing Tips Provided by* Stephen Aron with IFE[87]

---

[87] http://bit.ly/IFEshipping

View an example

INVENTORY PACK LIST **at:**

http://bit.ly/packinglistec

ECUADOR'S CUSTOMS REGULATIONS*

CONTAINER SHIPMENTS:

Please note that the information provided is subject to change at any time by the Customs authorities.

HOUSEHOLD GOODS AND PERSONAL EFFECTS

These are new or used goods such as appliances, clothing, kitchen and bathroom items, dining, living and bedroom furniture, home appliances, computers, ornaments, paintings, china, books, household tools and other items that have been acquired before moving to Ecuador. There is no restriction on the total value of household goods, but if Customs Inspectors determine that any item inventoried is not for personal use, taxable duties will apply.

WORK EQUIPMENT

These are new or used sets of tools, instruments and/or professional equipment for the production of work or trade, linked or not to the activity, profession or occupation of the shipper or family member. This also means any portable or stationery tools, equipment, instruments, structures or machinery that can be considered work related.

In the event that the work equipment exceeds thirty thousand dollars (USD $30,000), the immigrant must submit a draft BUSINESS INVESTMENT IN ECUADOR AND THE RESPECTIVE WORK PERMISSION.

DUTIABLE/RESTRICTED ITEMS

- New items and shipments in excess of a certain valuation may be subject to duties

- Clothing allowance - see below - excess of allowance will incur a Customs tax

- Only three bottles of liquor are allowed in a container - no tobacco

- For electronics and appliances - check with Ecuador Shipping for specific details prior to shipping

CLOTHING

Each family member is allowed up to 200kilos (440lbs) for clothing, footwear and personal accessories. Any excess will incur a customs tax. These items must be packed separately and correspond in size to each family member. You are not allowed to ship clothes that do not belong to you or your family even if you intend to donate clothes in Ecuador, this will cause delays and extra fees.

PROHIBITED ITEMS

- Firearms and ammunitions

- Stun guns, archery or weaponry

- Drugs and narcotics

- Pornographic material

- Raw material (not treated wood, or food that is not properly packaged)

- Unpackaged foodstuff and live plants

- Cell phones

- Appliances using refrigerant R12-R15

- Cleaning products

- Creams, colognes, perfumes and cosmetics

- Significant amounts of textiles, fabric (no more than 5 yards)

DOCUMENTS REQUIRED TO SHIP A CONTAINER

- Passport with permanent residency or work visa
- Statement from owner that contents of shipment are for personal use and will not be sold for 5 years.
- Completed Inventory Value Packing list translated into Spanish and notarized in Ecuador
- Immigrant Certificate valid for Customs clearance obtained in Ecuador (for returning Ecuadorians).
- Commitment in writing that articles brought into the country duty-free will only be used for personal use and not for resale.
- Standard documentation is included in fees quoted by Ecuador Shipping. Additional fees may apply if you request specialized shipping services.

NOTE

   U.S. citizens in Ecuador are required to carry identification including proof of US citizenship at all times. If you are stopped and cannot present evidence of identity and legal status in Ecuador, it is possible that you could be arrested and deported. Because of the frequency of passport theft, you should carry a photocopy of your passport and visa entry stamp and cedula, rather than the actual passport and identity card.

* *Provided by Ecuador Shipping*

Compare Ecuador with Costa Rica:

Becoming an Expat: Costa Rica is available for purchase now!

COMING SOON

Becoming an Expat: Thailand

Becoming an Expat: Brazil

Becoming an Expat: Mexico

visit:
www.Becominganexpat.com

✦To see changes in-between editions

✦For additional resources

✦Read our blog

✦To discover what we come up with next!

Cover Art

Deidre Hof

Editing

Lisa Bailey

Formatting

Shannon Enete

Photography

Cover photo: Shannon Enete

Made in the USA
Middletown, DE
27 January 2017